MW00641987

GOD'S BIBLE
— IN —
SPANISH

HOW GOD PRESERVED HIS WORDS
IN SPANISH THROUGH THE RVG

EMANUEL RODRIGUEZ

CHICK PUBLICATIONS
ONTARIO, CALIFORNIA 91761

Additional copies of this book are available from
Christian bookstores and distributors worldwide.

For a complete up-to-date list of distributors near you,
visit: www.chick.com/distrib.asp

To order a copy directly from the publisher,
call: (909) 987-0771.
Or visit: www.chick.com

GOD'S BIBLE IN SPANISH

HOW GOD PRESERVED HIS WORDS IN SPANISH THROUGH THE RVG

Published by:
CHICK PUBLICATIONS
PO Box 3500, Ontario, Calif. 91761-1019 USA
Tel: (909) 987-0771
Fax: (909) 941-8128
Web: www.chick.com/es
Email: postmaster@chick.com

Printed in the United States of America

ISBN: 978-0-7589-0764-6

FOREWORD

For years, we at Chick Publications wrestled with which Spanish Bible version we should use in our tracts for Spanish-speaking people because we found problems with all of them.

A few years ago one Spanish Bible version was sent to us, claiming to have fixed the corrupt Alexandrian errors. We almost went with it, but when we sent a copy to our professional Spanish translators, to our dismay, they found numerous mistakes. I was crestfallen.

At that point I despaired of finding a Spanish Bible that was as true in form and meaning to God's preserved Greek and Hebrew as the King James is in English.

But a couple of years ago, missionaries began encouraging us to consider the Reina-Valera Gómez (RVG) Bible. They were so polite and godly in their correspondence that we ordered some copies.

Then I asked our Spanish translators and various other Spanish speakers to read them and give me their thoughts, as I checked my copy of the RVG.

The results were quite positive. Brother Humberto was

humble enough to correct the few errors we found at that earlier stage. "After all," he said, "it is not my Bible." That has been his attitude in all the time I have come to know him.

It is exciting that Brother Gómez spent several years cleaning up the text, in conjunction with other Bible-believers in thirteen countries. Even when Brother Gómez only had a draft copy, the people received the RVG 2004 as the best Bible they had ever seen, and offered themselves to help in the proofreading process.

In this way many Christians were able to read and re-read the RVG 2004 and show him anything that still needed to be corrected to match God's preserved words.

Now the process has been completed. The RVG 2010 is the result of over five years of careful review from many qualified scholars and Bible-believers of all sorts.

All these Christians have seen that the form of Spanish communicates well in all those diverse countries, without bias or misunderstanding. The product of Gómez's work, checked by the countless brothers and sisters under his leadership, is called the Reina-Valera Gómez Bible.

We were overjoyed. As a result, we at Chick Publications worked hard to change the scriptures in our Spanish tracts to use the RVG 2010. And any future Spanish literature from Chick Publications will also quote the RVG 2010.

In short, I fully and enthusiastically endorse the Reina-Valera Gómez Bible as God's preserved words in Spanish.

David W. Daniels
Research Consultant, Chick Publications

PREFACE

Due to my close relationship to this issue, some have assumed that I was one of Dr. Humberto Gómez's collaborators in his translation work. But this is not so. I have simply been a bystander and a supporter.

Men much better than myself, with a deep command of the language and the culture of their native lands aided Dr. Gómez in his goal of purifying the Spanish text.

Veteran Bible-believing missionaries who are fluent in the language have also participated. I simply could not hold a candle to these men of God. I thank God for every one of them.

However, I tried to contribute what I could. I had the privilege to help Dr. Gómez in formatting the template of the bilingual edition of the RVG with the King James Version (KJV) parallel to it.

What a joy to see the success of this parallel edition. Hispanic Bible-believers around the world are excited to have a copy of God's perfectly preserved words in both Spanish and English in one volume.

During my time in Dr. Gómez's home in Mexico while we worked alongside each other on the parallel template, I got to see firsthand the passion, determination, and diligence by which he operated.

His work ethic is tireless and manifests an obsession with completing the task that he believes with all his heart that God has laid before him for the sake of his people.

I also tried to contribute by way of educating others as to what Dr. Gómez and his collaborators had done. Hence, this book.

This book is not meant to be a thorough dissertation on subjects of Bibliology such as the verbal, plenary inspiration and preservation of the scriptures. Nor did I discuss every detail concerning the transmission of the texts involved. Although these topics are mentioned, it is in more of a touch-and-go fashion.

The purpose of this book is simply to reveal the history behind the making of the Reina-Valera Gómez Bible and to express the true motives and desires that drove this work. In this regard, I have tried to get straight to the point.

As with anything else in life, Dr. Gómez's work has not been without its critics. Dr. Gómez and his collaborators were misrepresented, misjudged, and falsely accused on numerous occasions.

No good work will ever go unchallenged, which is why I appreciate the good attitude Dr. Gómez and his collaborators maintained concerning their critics. I only wish that I could be as composed.

Many times upon witnessing the invective of those moved

with envy who made it their mission to try to discredit Dr. Gómez's work at all cost, I desired some type of verbal or literary retribution in return.

But every time, Dr. Gómez reminded me that "it's not about us, it's about the Lord and His words." Perhaps someday I, too, will be able to exhibit this same kind of humility and meekness when dealing with those of the opposing viewpoint.

Nevertheless, I pray that this book will be used, despite my shortcomings and limitations, to enlighten sincere inquirers concerning the making of the Reina-Valera Gómez Bible.

It has been a privilege to work with a veteran soldier of the Lord like Dr. Gómez in producing this book. He was gracious to spend as much time as I desired to answer all of my questions as I interviewed him for many hours over the phone, via email and instant messenger, and in person. I am honored to tell his story.

I tried my best to put the message of Dr. Gómez into written form. I pray that my efforts will do at least a fraction of justice to the magnitude of Dr. Gómez's work.

I trust that the genuineness of his heart and spirit, as well as his perseverance in the daunting task of Bible revision, will inspire many in their pursuit to win the Spanish-speaking world to the Lord Jesus Christ.

Your servant and fellow-soldier in Christ,
Emanuel Rodriguez
Missionary to Puerto Rico
www.4thesaviour.com

Contents

CHAPTER 3

The Necessity of Further Revision 43

CHAPTER 4

Principles of the Reina-Valera Gómez Revision 67

CHAPTER 5

The Making of the Reina-Valera Gómez Bible 89

CHAPTER 6

Removing Hell from the Bible 119

INTRODUCTION

For several years I have followed with intensity the controversy of the Spanish Bible. My great concern over this issue stems from a passion to see my own people, Hispanic people, come to the saving knowledge of the Lord Jesus Christ. However, for me to lead souls to Christ I need a Bible. I have learned that not just any Bible will do. I want a Bible that is completely accurate, with nothing missing.

The Lord Himself said:

> Man shall not live by bread alone, but by every
> word that proceedeth out of the mouth of
> God.[1]

Therefore, in order for a Bible to be correct it must have *every word of God* accurately translated in the receptor language. Accuracy demands that there must be no omissions, additions, or alterations to God's holy words.

In English, I do not hesitate to say that we have such a Bible in the King James Bible.

---

1) Matthew 4:4.

In Spanish, I do not hesitate to say that in 1602 God provided the Spanish-speaking world essentially the same thing that He eventually provided the English-speaking world – His precious words in the Reina-Valera Bible.

Despite many setbacks and disruptions due to the opposition of the Roman Catholic church, Casiodoro de Reina completed the first entire Bible in Spanish in 1569.

God raised up Reina's friend, Cipriano de Valera, to revise this initial Spanish translation. But despite Valera's meticulous work of twenty years, there was still more work to be done.

As we will see, Valera allowed for the further revision of his work. Nevertheless, thanks to the courageous efforts of Reina and Valera, the Spanish world was well on its way to having a completely accurate Spanish Bible.

However, after 1602, modernistic and ecumenical Bible societies got their hands on our Received Text-based Protestant Bible in Spanish and corrupted it by incorporating Alexandrian Critical Texts.

This was most unfortunate.

Many revisions were done based upon the principles of modern day textual criticism but only two were ever widely circulated. The Reina-Valera 1909 and the Reina-Valera 1960 revisions eventually became the only two realistic options for Spanish-speaking Christians.

A revision produced in 1865, but never widely circulated, resurfaced in recent years and was republished by a small group of supporters who claimed it was more accurate than the 1909 and 1960 revisions.

For several years, I was puzzled over which Spanish Bible I should use. They all had problems. I prayed that God would raise up some brave Hispanic Bible believer to revise the Reina-Valera Bible by replacing the corruptions with pure readings that reflected the Received Texts and agreed with the King James Bible.

Little did I realize that I was not alone in my concerns.

I began to look into different projects that attempted to provide a more pure Spanish Bible. The more I investigated, the more I began to realize that there was a bit of an uproar within the Hispanic Fundamentalist ranks over this issue. These different revision projects were stirring up a heated controversy.

At first, I did not know what to make of all this. All I knew was that God had called me to preach the Gospel to Hispanic souls. And no matter who disapproved, I needed to use a Spanish Bible in which I could have full confidence in every word.[2]

GOD ANSWERED MY PRAYER

As God is my witness, I prayed for years that God would direct my paths as to which of these projects I should support, *if any*. I believe in recent years God has answered my prayers, as well as the similar prayers of many others.

For nearly a decade, Dr. Humberto Gómez and his collaborators worked hard to produce a revision of the Spanish Bible that is completely based upon the Received Texts and equivalent to the King James Bible.

---

2) Matthew 4:4.

He released the first draft of his work in 2004. Several other drafts were published after that, culminating with the final version, the RVG 2010.

This Bible has been adopted by Bible-believing Spanish-speaking brethren all over the world, in countries such as Spain, Peru, Guatemala, Chile, Argentina, Costa Rica, Paraguay, Panama, Uruguay, Ecuador, Belize, and the Dominican Republic.

It has also been adopted by Spanish ministries all over Mexico, as well as by many Spanish ministries in the United States. Ministers and laymen around the world rejoice to finally have a Spanish Bible in their hands that is much more accurate and in accordance to the Received Texts.

After many sleepless nights while investigating these matters, I am more than convinced that this is indeed a work of God. I wholeheartedly support Dr. Gómez's revision of the Spanish Bible.

As you will see, Bible believers around the world are also arriving at this same conclusion. For the remainder of this book, I wish to share with you the story of how God has preserved His holy words in Spanish through the Reina-Valera Gómez Bible.

CHAPTER 1

About Dr. Humberto Gómez

Dr. Humberto Gómez was born in Monterrey, Mexico on Sept. 17, 1952. He is the second oldest of five sons. He also has two older sisters. His father worked as a police officer in Mexico and provided well for the Gómez family.

Unfortunately, Brother Humberto was only 8 years old when his father died. His mother was forced to work and provide for the rest of the family.

She decided not to marry again. This meant that the burden to take care of her children rested totally upon her shoulders. After selling everything they had, the Gómez family lived a life of poverty in Mexico.

Mrs. Gómez would work jobs that normally only men would do such as digging ditches and painting houses. She also worked in the cotton fields in Matamoros, Mexico. The cotton industry was big in those days.

As a little boy, Humberto watched his mother carry large sacks of cotton. She would do anything to take care of her seven children. No doubt her work ethic, motivated by her love for her children, made a lasting impression upon Brother Humberto Gómez.

Brother Gómez and his older brother, Bernardo, also worked after school to help their hard-working mother. They worked in the streets shining shoes, selling gum, newspapers, and anything else they could do to help their mother take care of the family. Brother Gómez reminisces:

> I remember how good it felt to come home
> with a pocket full of change to give to my
> mother. It was a joy to be able to help my
> mother considering the great burden she car-
> ried and the sacrifices she made for us.

TROUBLE AND PRISON

But as he worked on the streets, Brother Gómez ran into older boys who introduced him to a life of trouble. At an early age, they introduced him to alcohol, stealing, cheating, fighting, and every other type of wickedness that goes along with the street life. His life went swiftly downhill as he spent much time in and out of prison.

Unfortunately, his brothers also went down this same path of mischief and street life. They started using and selling drugs. They became criminals. I will refrain from sharing the details of some of the violent crimes that the Gómez brothers were involved in. Needless to say, their lives were in a horrible mess.

There was an instance when four of them were in prison at the same time. Brother Gómez explains:

> As you can imagine our sinful behavior brought a lot of pain and sorrow upon our mother who sacrificed so much to take care of us.

When Brother Gómez was released from prison at the age of nineteen, he was so ashamed of his miserable life that he did not want to go home. But it was a good thing he did. Little did he realize what he would encounter that day. Brother Gómez testifies:

> I was too embarrassed to face my mother and the reality of my wickedness. I did not know what to do or where to turn. I had nothing to live for. I was sick of this life. But I had nowhere else to go so that day I returned home. As I sat outside my mother's house on a dilapidated bench – much like my life – a stranger carrying a Bible visited. This was the first time I ever saw a Bible. Like most Mexicans, we were Catholics. But I never even knew that such a Book existed.

This visitor was a Mexican preacher who was working with an American missionary from Denver, Colorado. This faithful soul winner opened his Bible and preached to young Humberto the glorious Gospel of Jesus Christ. Brother Gómez recalls:

> For the first time in my life, I heard that God loved me despite my wickedness. Every time I ever heard about God I was under the impres-

sion that God hated me and was going to do
nothing but punish me for my evil ways.

Though the message of God's judgment upon sinners
is true, Brother Gómez learned that God's love and mercy
upon sinners who turn to Him was just as true. Brother
Gómez further elaborates:

> My religion never taught me that God was
> willing to save a wretch like me. They never
> told me that if I would put my faith in the
> blood that Christ shed for me on the cross
> that, not only would He save me from an
> eternity in hell, but He would change my life.
> When I heard all this, the message of God's
> love for me was so unbelievable that I did not
> get saved at that moment. It was too hard for
> me to comprehend that God could forgive
> someone like me.

But that day, a seed was sown in his heart. And from
that day on, the message of that Mexican soul winner stuck
in Brother Gómez's heart, and echoed in his mind over and
over again.

HUMBERTO GÓMEZ
GETS SAVED

Finally, six months later, in 1971, Humberto Gómez
surrendered to the convicting power of the Holy Ghost and
received Christ as his personal Saviour! As he puts it, "It was
the greatest day of my life!" Praise the Lord!

As a newborn Christian, the first thing he did was run

home to tell his mother the good news. In front of his mother he dropped to his knees on the dirt floor and said:

> Mom, I know that I have caused you a lot of grief and pain with my wickedness. But something happened to me today. I asked Jesus to save me. And He did. He has changed my life. And I ask you to forgive me for all the grief I caused you.

Mrs. Gómez's first reaction was one of skepticism, for she was a Catholic and this type of talk from her son sounded strange to her. She thought he had gone crazy. She responded, "Don't tell me you became a Protestant."

Brother Gómez tried to explain to her that it wasn't about religion but that he had simply become a born again Christian. But considering her son's troublesome lifestyle up to that point, all this was so odd that it took her a while to understand what had happened.

FAMILY MEMBERS GET SAVED

Brother Gómez began witnessing to the rest of his brothers and sisters. One by one, they each trusted Christ as their Saviour. As Mrs. Gómez observed the drastic change in her son's life, God also started working in her heart and she eventually got saved (she is now in heaven).

Today all of the Gómez family is in church and serving God. All five of the Gómez brothers became preachers. Most of their sons and nephews have also answered the call to preach. Some of them now pastor churches in Mexico.

And now some of their grandchildren have experienced

the call of God in their lives to preach the Gospel as well. God has done a marvelous work in the Gómez family.

To God be the glory!

THE CALL TO PREACH

About six months after his conversion in 1972, God called Brother Gómez to preach. For nearly forty years, he has traveled throughout Mexico, preaching the Gospel of the Lord Jesus Christ. God has used Dr. Gómez to help establish local churches throughout Mexico.

His brothers, along with their sons and nephews, are also responsible for planting many Bible-believing churches in Mexico.

The Gómez brothers have started two Bible institutes in Mexico, where nationals are being trained for the ministry. Graduates from these schools are also planting churches all over their country. Some of these nationals have even surrendered to leave Mexico and travel to other countries as church planting missionaries.

Several years ago, God also opened a door for Dr. Gómez to work with the Aztec Indians. About twenty local churches among the Aztec Indians have been established in the mountains of Mexico as a result of Dr. Gómez's ministry.

He also has a ministry reaching men in the fishing villages with the Gospel. As Dr. Gómez testifies, "We have seen God do a great work here amongst our people!"

In addition to his work in Mexico, Dr. Gómez has preached in many Spanish-speaking countries such as Spain, Cuba, Peru, Paraguay, Guatemala, Chile, and others. Due to his many years of faithful service in the work of missions around the world, today he is in high demand as a missions conference speaker in the U. S.

INTRODUCTION TO THE BIBLE VERSION ISSUE

Brother Gómez was led to the Lord with a 1909 Antigua edition of the Reina-Valera Bible. And this was the Bible he used for the gospel ministry for over thirty years. To this day, this Bible is dear to his heart.

Dr. Gómez never questioned the accuracy of his Spanish Bible until he was confronted about a few passages by a preacher friend named Jack Wood, who was the pastor of Shady Acres Baptist Church in Houston, Texas for many years, before going on to be with the Lord.

Jack Wood was a great man of God known for his candid style of preaching, his love for the Mexican people, and a zeal in raising funds to support missionaries around the world. He was a great influence upon Dr. Gómez and many other Mexican preachers. Many Mexican pastors affectionately referred to him as "a white Mexican."

One day in the early eighties Brother Wood asked Dr. Gómez to turn to Dan. 3:25 and compare it with his English King James Bible. To Brother Gómez's surprise they read differently. The KJV said:

…the form of the fourth is like *the Son of God.*

The 1909 Antigua version of the Reina-Valera Bible read, "el parecer del cuarto es semejante á hijo de los dioses" which is translated:

...the form of the fourth is like unto *a son of the gods.*

Obviously, there is a big difference between *"the Son of God"* and *"a son of the gods."*

Dr. Gómez recalls his feelings upon this discovery:

My first reaction to this revelation was defensive. I even felt offended. I tried to explain to Brother Wood why I believed the rendering was correct in my Bible.

I gave him the typical explanation that most preachers give in defense of Daniel 3:25 in the modern versions. I said that Nebuchadnezzar was lost and therefore he could not have recognized the Son of God.

But this was ignoring the fact that Nebuchadnezzar did not write the book of Daniel. The book was penned by Daniel under the guidance of the Holy Ghost.

As I further looked into the matter I realized the error of how Daniel 3:25 was rendered in my Spanish Bible. Brother Wood also showed me other passages that contradicted the KJV. This sparked an interest to learn English so that I could compare the Spanish Bible and the KJV for myself. I studied the differences and over the years compiled notes of my research. The more I researched the differences between my Bible and the KJV, the more God opened my eyes to the reality of the corrupt Alexan-

drian texts and their influence upon Bibles in
every language.

I knew that something needed to be done about
this problem. I wrestled with the idea of revising the Spanish Bible for many years before
I actually took on the task. I asked Brother
Wood in those days for his advice. He said,
"Now is not the time. But in due time, God
will provide everything you need."

Dr. Gómez took Brother Wood's advice to wait on the
Lord to reveal the right time to take on the task of revising
the Spanish Bible. Meanwhile, he continued studying the
Bible text issue and compiling notes concerning the differences between his Spanish Bible and the KJV.

WORK ON THE RVG BEGINS

After many years of studying, praying and preparing,
Dr. Gómez felt in his heart that it was indeed God's will for
him to take on the challenge of purifying the Reina-Valera
text. Dr. Gómez explains:

I prayed many years seeking God's direction in
regards to what I could do to help my people
have a more pure Spanish Bible. Finally, the
day came when I could wait no longer and
with much fear and trembling we took on the
enormous task of revising our Spanish Bible.

Dr. Gómez is living proof of what God can do with a
man who totally surrenders his life to the Lord. Here is a
man who God delivered from the gutters of sin and not only

made him a born again Christian, but made him a preacher of the Gospel of Jesus Christ, a successful church planter, and now a Bible reviser.

> For ye see your calling, brethren, how that not many wise men after the flesh, not many mighty, not many noble, are called: But God hath chosen the foolish things of the world to confound the wise; and God hath chosen the weak things of the world to confound the things which are mighty; And base things of the world, and things which are despised, hath God chosen, yea, and things which are not, to bring to nought things that are: That no flesh should glory in his presence.[3]

Who is better to revise the Spanish Bible than a man who is a native Hispanic, a true Bible-believer, and even more importantly one who has a fervent love for his own people, as proven by his nearly forty years of serving them with the Gospel?

The RVG 2010 is not merely a work of scholarship, though a work of scholarship it is, but it is the result of a love of God and His people.

---

3) 1 Corinthians 1:26-29.

CHAPTER 2

A Brief History of the Reina-Valera Bible

In order to understand the necessity of the Reina-Valera Gómez revision, understanding the history behind the traditional Spanish Bible text is paramount. This chapter provides a brief historical account of the process by which the Reina-Valera Bible came about.

Many portions of the Bible were translated into Castilian before Casiodoro de Reina first began his translation of the scriptures into Spanish. This chapter will discuss the major factors that relate to the making of the Reina-Valera Bible.

THE FERRARA BIBLE

The first translation of the entire Hebrew Old Testament into Spanish was done in 1553 by two Spanish-speaking Jews named Duarte Pinel (aka Abraham Ben Salomon Usque) and Geronimo de Vargas (aka Yom Tob Levi Atias).

After dedicating their translation to Ercole II d'Este, the Duke of Ferrara, it became known as the Ferrara Bible. It was printed by a Jewish press in Ferrara, Italy, for circulation among the Spanish-speaking Jews that lived in Spain.

This Spanish Old Testament was an extremely literal word-for-word translation of the Hebrew Masoretic text (which is also the underlying basis for the Old Testament in the King James Version). The books of the Old Testament were arranged according to the traditional Hebrew canon. Concerning the highly literal style of this translation, it is stated in the *Cambridge History of the Bible:*

> The translation was made word-for-word from the Hebrew, and its syntax is therefore peculiar. The abundant archaisms and 'intolerable Hebraisms'- the consequence of its compilation, perhaps, from manuscripts used for instructional purposes in medieval Spanish synagogues, add to the bizarre character.
>
> Nevertheless, it sometimes has (as the preface states) "the gravity that antiquity often has." This frankly Jewish Bible gave immense help to later translators of the Old Testament, Catholic and Protestant alike. For it was used both by Reyna in the sixteenth century and by Father Scio de San Miguel in the eighteenth...
>
> There are many later editions of the Ferrara Bible, mostly published for the Jews at Amsterdam.[4]

---

4) *Cambridge History of the Bible*, p. 127.

This Spanish Old Testament was not without its faults however. Some Messianic passages such as Isaiah 9:6 were tampered with. Fortunately, Reina's text did not reflect these tampered passages.

FRANCISCO DE ENZINAS

Francisco de Enzinas (1520-1553) was born in a wealthy family. His parents sent him and his two brothers, Jayme and Juan, to Louvain University in Belgium. It was there that all three brothers were saved and rejected Roman Catholicism. The Spanish Inquisition was in full swing in those days and it wasn't long before the Inquisitors captured Juan and burned him at the stake.

That the Protestant Reformation had much influence upon Francisco de Enzinas is evident by his friendship with Philip Melancthon, the famed assistant of Martin Luther. Enzinas lived with Melancthon in Wittenberg for a while.

Enzinas eventually mastered the Greek language, and at the suggestion of Melancthon, he soon put his knowledge of Greek to work by translating the New Testament into Spanish using the Greek text of Desiderius Erasmus.

It was printed in Antwerp in 1543. The title was "El Nuevo Testamento, o sea, el Nuevo Pacto de Nuestro Único Redentor y Salvador Jesucristo, traducido del Griego al Castellano," which means "The New Testament, that is, the New Covenant of our Only Redeemer and Saviour Jesus Christ, translated from the Greek to the Castilian language."

On November 24th, 1543, Francisco de Enzinas presented his Spanish New Testament to the Emperor Charles

V in Brussels, hoping to receive approval for distribution. Charles V appeared to be open-minded to Enzinas' work and even offered his endorsement of it if upon examination his New Testament was found to be acceptable.

The Emperor gave a copy to his confessor, Pedro de Soto, for examination. But after no short period of time, Pedro de Soto reported back with a stern rebuke rather than approval. The emperor's confessor labeled Enzinas an enemy of religion and a traitor to his country. As a result, Enzinas was imprisoned by the Catholic inquisitors with the charge of heresy.

The "heresy" that Enzinas was accused of involved the words "New Covenant" in the title of his New Testament. Such terminology was labeled by the Catholics as "Lutheranism." The words "Only Redeemer and Saviour" also infuriated the Catholic church because of its exclusion of the Pope.

But the straw that broke the camel's back was the passages that Enzinas had capitalized in bold letters which dealt with the doctrine of justification by faith alone such as Romans 3:22 and 28.

During his fifteen months in prison, Francisco was visited by his family only to be condemned as one who brought a reproach upon their name.

He was able to escape, however, before the Inquisitors could kill him and he fled to Antwerp.

He eventually moved to England, where he served as a Greek instructor at Cambridge. In 1553, Enzinas died of the plague in Strasbourg.

ERASMUS AND HIS
GREEK NEW TESTAMENT

By this time Erasmus' Greek text had already become the basis for Luther's German translation and William Tyndale's English translation.

It eventually became the foundation for many other Protestant translations, including the Spanish texts mentioned in this chapter such as Enzinas' text.

A famous saying is:

Erasmus laid the egg that Luther hatched.

Thus, Erasmus' Greek text spearheaded a movement of Bible translating that characterized the Protestant Reformation in a time when the common man began looking more towards the scriptures for truth than the Roman Catholic church.

It was this demand all over Europe for access to the scriptures that fueled the Protestant Reformation. And while it is technically true that Erasmus was a Catholic, God greatly used his outspokenness against the corruptions of the Catholic church, as well as his writings, to stir much dissent against the Papal institution. But it was Erasmus' Greek New Testament that really lit the fuse of Protestantism on fire.

For the word of God is quick, and powerful, and sharper than any twoedged sword...[5]

Erasmus' Greek text became the first in a pure line of revisions of the Greek New Testament that we now know as the Textus Receptus.

---

5) Hebrews 4:12.

THE OPPOSITION OF
THE CATHOLIC CHURCH

It was because of the influence of Francisco de Enzinas and other Protestant Reformers who were on a mission to get the word of God into the respective languages of the common people throughout Europe that the Roman Catholic Church printed their first Index of the Spanish Inquisition in Toledo, Spain in 1551.

In the Index, it was declared illegal for anyone to translate the scriptures without the approval of the Catholic church. They prohibited the:

> ...Bible in Castilian romance or in any other vulgar tongue, the Spanish New testament of Francisco de Enzinas and those "Old and New testaments, Gospels, Epistles and Prophecies and any other books of Holy Scripture in Castilian romance, French or Flemish or any other tongue which have prefaces, notes or glosses that reveal erroneous doctrines repugnant or contrary to our holy Catholic faith or to the sacraments of Holy Mother Church."

In 1559, another Index was issued which also prohibited:

> The Bible in our vernacular or in any other, wholly or in part, unless it be in Hebrew, Chaldean, Greek or Latin... And because there are some pieces of Gospels and Epistles of St. Paul and other parts of the New Testament in the Castilian vernacular both printed and in manuscript from which certain objectionable con-

sequences have followed, we order such books
and treatises to be shown and handed over
to the Holy Office [of the Catholic church],
whether or not they bear their authors' names,
until the Council of the Holy General Inquisition shall determine otherwise.

Non-conformity to the Index of the Roman Catholic
church rendered severe consequences. But God's soldiers
marched on, getting the word of God to the common people,
choosing to fear and obey God rather than man.

JUAN PEREZ DE PINEDA

Another man burdened with the desire to get the word
of God to his people was Juan Perez de Pineda (1490-1567).
He was educated in Seville, Spain, where he received a Doctorate in Divinity. Like Enzinas, he was greatly influenced
by Protestant thought, having been a member of a small
Protestant church in Seville.

After fleeing from Inquisitors of Spain, he eventually
became a member of a panel of pastors that worked with
the famous John Calvin in Geneva. From 1556-1560 he
published many works that promoted Protestant ideas and
doctrines to be smuggled into Spain.

Perez is responsible for translating the second complete
New Testament in Spanish by a Protestant. For his work he
also used Erasmus' Greek text as the basis and relied heavily upon the New Testament of Enzinas. Juan Perez's New
Testament was published in Geneva in 1556. He also had
the book of Psalms published in 1557.

In 1556, John Calvin took a team of delegates with him to Frankfurt to help settle a dispute over the observance of Holy Communion in a church. Juan Perez was one of Calvin's delegates.

After the controversy was dealt with, Calvin and his delegates returned to Geneva but Juan remained in Frankfurt until June of 1558. While there, he started a fund with plans of publishing the entire Bible in Spanish. Pineda was not able to accomplish this goal but the funds he raised later aided the translator, Casiodoro de Reina.

The Catholic Inquisitors never were able to capture Juan Perez de Pineda so they had to settle for burning a sculptured image of him in Seville in 1560. Perez died in Paris of a disease in 1567. He left behind all of his fortune for the printing of the Spanish Bible, no doubt laying up treasure for himself in heaven.

JULIAN THE LITTLE

While Europe was being turned upside down through the preaching of Bible-believing non-conformists such as the Waldenses and Albigenses (which eventually led to the dissension of the Protestant Reformers), God was doing a great work among the monks and members of a monastery known as San Isidro del Campo, located in Santiponce, near Seville, Spain.

The Superior of this monastery was Dr. Blanco Garcia Arias. Dr. Blanco was greatly influenced by the preaching of the Waldenses and their Old Latin Bible (not to be confused with the corrupt Catholic Latin Vulgate of Jerome,) which was a very pure version of God's words with a manuscript trail that can be traced back to the Apostolic age.

These Old Latin Bibles also serve as some of the greatest manuscript evidence for the authenticity of the Johannine Comma (1 John 5:7).

Thanks to the courageous exploits of another Protestant named Julian Hernandez, aka Julian the Little, copies of both Enzinas' and Juan Perez's New Testaments, as well as much literature promoting Protestant teachings, were smuggled into this monastery in cases of wine.

These works had a great effect on the monks in that monastery, most especially Casiodoro de Reina.

Unfortunately, Julian was betrayed by a supposed friend and imprisoned for his "crime" of Bible smuggling. He was brutally tortured by the Catholic Inquisitors.

After three years of remaining firm in the faith despite the persecution, refusing to denounce his convictions, Julian was burned alive at the stake.

The Spanish world owes its gratitude to such heroes of the faith such as Julian Hernandez. Though he was physically of small stature, thus his nickname (Julian the Little), he was a giant in the faith.

The Catholic church confiscated and burned the works that Julian Hernandez possessed. But it was too late. The scriptures and Protestant literature, as well as the teaching of Dr. Blanco Garcia Arias, had already touched the heart of another monk in the monastery in Seville —the great Casiodoro de Reina. A fire in his soul was already lit for translating the entire Bible into Spanish.

CASIODORO DE REINA

Casiodoro de Reina (1520-1594), a native of Seville, Spain, was probably the most influential of all the monks at the monastery in Seville during the revival that took place there.

Like all other Protestants who took a stand against the Catholic church, he also became a target of the wrath of the murderous Inquisitors.

Eventually Reina fled Spain, never to return. Twenty-one other monks were not so fortunate, and were burned at the stake in 1559.

That same year Reina took on the pastorate of a group of Protestants in London who had also fled Spain. But again, the Catholic church pursued him as they brought their crusade of persecution to England. So Reina fled London.

He moved to Geneva and joined himself to a Spanish congregation pastored by Juan Perez de Pineda. Perez was still in Frankfurt during Reina's arrival to Geneva.

It wasn't long before the Spaniards in Geneva began looking to Reina for leadership during Juan Perez's absence. So influential was Casiodoro de Reina amongst these Spanish Protestants that he became known as the "The Moses of the Spaniards."

However, Reina greatly disagreed with John Calvin and his method of leadership in Geneva. Reina spoke out against Calvin in Geneva for the burning of Servetus at the stake. He referred to Geneva as "a new Rome." Eventually, Reina and several other fellow-monks who also served at San Isidoro left Geneva and moved to Frankfurt.

Concerning this period in Reina's life, in an article entitled *The Reina-Valera Bible: From Dream to Reality* by Jorge A. Gonzalez, the author offers some interesting speculation:

> It is not certain whether Reina and Perez met at this time in Frankfurt or in Geneva. It is most probable, however, that the two discussed, some time during this period, the possibility of publishing the Bible in Spanish, for it is from this time that Reina dates the beginning of his work on the Scriptures, as can be seen from the preface of his "Bear Bible" and from the autograph dedicatory of the copy which he donated to the University of Basel.

Reina originally only planned on translating the Old Testament, relying heavily upon the Ferrara Bible that was circulating amongst the Jews in Spain. His plan was to join the New Testament of Juan de Pineda with his translation of the Old Testament.

But on April 6, 1568, Phillip II ordered his ambassador in France to burn all copies of Juan de Pineda's New Testament. So Reina was forced to translate his own New Testament, leaning much upon the text of Enzinas. He did, however, receive the funds that Pineda raised for the publishing of the Spanish Bible.

During Reina's work of translating the scriptures he was constantly pursued by the Catholic Inquisitors and a price was placed on his head. He was labeled a heretic, a criminal, and was even accused of being a Sodomite by the Catholic church.

Reina constantly fled from town to town… Antwerp, Frankfurt, Orleans, Bergerac, and others. But as a good soldier of Jesus Christ he endured such hardships and remained focused on his mission to translate the entire Bible into Spanish.

Finally he settled down in Basle, Switzerland, where he completed the first translation of the entire Bible in Spanish in 1569. It is hailed by historians as "the greatest literary triumph in Spanish history."

However, it was labeled by the Roman Catholic church as "a most dangerous edition of the Bible." But Satan and his cohorts of Rome could not stop the word of God.

Reina's Bible was known as "The Bear Bible" or "La Biblia del Oso," for on the title page was a picture of a bear retrieving honey from a tree.

After completing his translation of the Bible, Casiodoro de Reina pastored a Spanish church in Antwerp for the next 16 years. He died in 1594. But there was yet more work to be done.

CIPRIANO DE VALERA

Because of the disruptive pursuits by the Roman Catholic church that forced Reina to live a transient life, his translation of the Spanish Bible was done hurriedly. Thus it was still in need of revision.

The man God raised up to perform this job was a personal friend of Reina named Cipriano de Valera (1532-?). Valera was also a monk at the San Isidro del Campo Monastery. He probably fled at the same time as Reina in 1557. And like Reina, Cipriano spent some time in Geneva working with John Calvin.

Cipriano had a fervent desire for the ministry, so he eventually moved to England to study at the University of Cambridge.

He became an expert in ten different languages. Due to this mastery of languages he made a name for himself as an instructor at Oxford University. He had no lack of translating experience, as evidenced by his translation of John Calvin's Institutes.

He also was known for writing a booklet entitled "El Papa y La Misa" (The Pope and the Mass) in which he vehemently rebuked the pagan practices of Rome. But he is most known for his work on the Spanish Bible.

Cipriano de Valera started his work of revising Reina's translation in 1582. He finished and published his final product in 1602. That was twenty years of his life that he invested into the word of God for the Spanish-speaking people.

Valera called this revision The Second Edition. On the front page of his revision is a picture of two men, one sowing seed and the other watering the seed. Below the picture is the verse:

> I have planted, Apollos watered; but God gave
> the increase.[6]

The Hispanic world is indebted to these great men of God for whom this epic version of the scriptures is named: The

---

6) 1 Corinthians 3:6.

Reina-Valera Bible, a heritage handed down from Almighty
God to the Spanish-speaking world.

> Every good gift and every perfect gift is from
> above, and cometh down from the Father of
> lights, with whom is no variableness, neither
> shadow of turning.[7]

---

7) James 1:17.

CHAPTER 3

The Necessity of
Further Revision

Despite his effort of twenty years, Cipriano de Valera knew there was more work to be done. In his preface he said:

> Oh that it would please God that by His infinite mercy He inspire in the heart of the King to mandate throughout his coasts the gathering of pious and learned men in the Hebrew and Greek tongues that they would view and review this translation of the Bible; whom with a sincere and pious desire, that desire to serve God and do good to their nation, that they compare and challenge it with the Hebrew text that God dictated to his holy Prophets before the coming of Christ, and with the Greek text that He Himself dictated to his holy Apostles and Evangelists after the coming of Christ in the flesh.

It was Valera's dream for "pious and learned men in the Hebrew and Greek tongues" throughout Europe to be gathered under the king's authority to translate an authorized Bible in Spanish. Unfortunately, due to the dominance of the Catholic church in Spain in those days, this never took place for the Spanish-speaking people.

Due to Spain's significant place of prominence in history, some have speculated that perhaps God intended to use Spain rather than England (where the King James Bible was translated) to be the headquarters for the gathering of Europe's greatest scholars and linguists to translate an authorized Bible.

Valera's 1602 text could have been the basis for such a team of Bible translators. Furthermore, perhaps Spanish rather than English would have become today's foremost universal language.

Whether this speculation is true or not, the fact is, it wasn't until the 1800s, when the Spanish Inquisition ended, that the Spanish Bible was available for any major revision without the fear of opposition from the Catholic church.

For remember, the outlawing of the Reina-Valera Bible remained in effect in Spanish speaking countries, most of which were (and still are) dominated by the Catholic church, until the Spanish Inquisition officially ended in 1834.

Due to the stronghold the Catholic church and their Inquisitors had upon Spain at that time, the influence of the Spanish Bible was somewhat put on hold and the influence of Bible-believing Christianity in Spain was extremely limited until the 19th century.

VALERA'S DESIRE FOR
TEXTUAL PURITY

In the preface of his revision, Valera reveals his philosophy concerning the translation of the Spanish Bible:

> Also we have taken out all that was added by
> the 70 interpreters [the LXX], or of the Vul-
> gate, that is not found in the Hebrew text…
> I say this, so that if someone confers with
> this version called the Vulgate, and does not
> find in this [version] everything that is in that
> one, no marvel. Because our intent was not to
> translate what men have added to the word of
> God, only what God has revealed in his Holy
> Scriptures…

Valera made it plain that he intended to purify Reina's 1569 translation by removing any readings based on the Greek Septuagint (LXX) and the Latin Vulgate that did not line up with the pure Hebrew text. This was his way of distinguishing purity from corruption.

The Septuagint was a Greek translation of the Old Testament that reflected the corrupt Alexandrian line of manuscripts that were tampered with by heretics.

Though we celebrate Reina's courage and initiative in giving the Spanish world the word of God, his translation philosophy was not without its flaws. One historian notes:

> In spite of his reverence for the Word of God,
> Casiodoro (Reina) had a critical attitude to the
> text of the Bible and was certainly no slavish
> literalist, but brought his historical and philo-

logical knowledge to bear on the problem of interpretation. Mention has already been made of Reina's understanding of Isaiah VII.14, "a virgin shall conceive..." as referring to the prophet's wife, and only by analogy to Mary, and a similar freedom may be discerned in the other annotations of Isaiah and Ezekiel.

In his Evangelium Johanis, he studiously avoids naming the author of Hebrews, writing several times "Autor epistolae ad Hebreos" and even separating the author from the Apostolic epistle writers... Reina admits allegorical interpretations, but firmly tries to see a passage as it struck the writer and those who first read it.[8]

Despite Valera's loyal friendship with Reina, they did not share the same translation philosophy. In fact, the nature of Valera's revision is evidence that he wished for the Spanish Bible to be free from Alexandrian corruption.

After twenty years of devotion to this cause, Valera came impressively close to producing a totally pure text. For the most part, his revision was based on the Traditional family of manuscripts (the Received Texts).

Dr. Rex Cobb, Director of Baptist Bible Translators Institute in Bowie, Texas, compared sixteen different Spanish Bible versions with the Textus Receptus. He concluded that Valera's revision had fewer than sixty departures from the Textus Receptus in the New Testament.

8) A. Gorgon Kinder, *Casiodoro de Reina: Spanish Reformer of the Sixteenth Century*, p. 90.

DEPARTURES FROM
THE TEXTUS RECEPTUS
IN THE 1602 VALERA

Carlos Donate, veteran missionary in Guatemala, prepared an article entitled *Examples of Departures from the Traditional Texts in the Original Reina and Valera Bibles* to be publicly read at the Dean Burgon Society's 30th Annual Conference in Oak Creek, Wisconsin on July 10, 2008. Some of the departures from the Textus Receptus in Valera's 1602 text that Donate addressed were:

1. Romans 1:16 – "of Christ" is omitted (these words existed in Enzina's and Pineda's New Testaments).
2. Matthew 24:2 – "Jesus" is omitted.
3. Luke 9:43 – "Jesus" is omitted.
4. Romans 15:17 – "Jesus" is omitted.
5. Acts 8:16 – "Lord" is omitted.
6. Acts 22:16 – "Lord" is omitted.
7. Exodus 15:11 – "among the gods" is omitted.
8. 1 Peter 2:2 – "grow unto salvation" was added.
9. Numbers 14:14 – "the Egyptians" was added.
10. Psalm 146:2 – "man" was added.
11. Job 7:4 – "my heart" was added.
12. Deuteronomy 32:25 and Joel 1:8 have "young woman" instead of "virgin."
13. Numbers 11:25 has "ceased" instead of "ceased not."

Donate pointed out several other passages but the point was to identify the need for further revision which, as we saw earlier, Valera himself allowed for in regards to his own text.

Basically, other than orthographical and some linguistic issues, all that was needed after 1602 was to correct the remaining departures from the Textus Receptus. We simply needed someone to pick up where Valera left off.

Unfortunately the opposite took place. Instead of improving and purifying Valera's text, modernistic Bible societies got involved with the Reina-Valera text and deliberately inserted more Alexandrian corruption to produce a Spanish Bible that reflected the Critical Texts more than the Traditional Texts that it was originally based upon.

This is why the current controversy exists over the Spanish Bible. Bible-believing Fundamentalists have complained for many years that the incorporation of the corrupt Critical Texts in revising Valera's work was a step backwards rather than forwards.

THE IDEA OF REVISION REVISITED

As stated earlier, the terror of the Spanish Inquisition began to die down in the early 1800s and was officially ended in 1834. For the most part, the Protestant Reformers had triumphed in their efforts to expose the corruption of the Roman Catholic church.

As the Catholic church's reign of terror began to fade, Protestants and Bible-believing Christians took advantage of the opportunity to take the Gospel to Spanish-speaking countries.

As a result, Christians began focusing their attention on Valera's Bible once again. An awareness of the need for further revision of the Spanish Bible began to develop. Over a century had gone by since Valera produced his great work of revision and so a need for linguistic and orthographical changes was in order.

THE CRITICAL TEXT MOVEMENT

Meanwhile, there was also a movement growing to produce Greek texts based upon the corrupt Alexandrian manuscripts in the 1800s that would eventually influence foreign Bible translations, including the Spanish Bible.

The two most famous Alexandrian manuscripts are the Vaticanus and Sinaiticus manuscripts which date back to the 4th century. Concerning these corrupt manuscripts, author Gary Miller explains:

> Modern Bible versions that are missing God's words go all the way back to manuscripts written in Alexandria, Egypt. Only about 44 of them have been found. Most are little scraps of paper or a few pages long. Three of them look like huge Bibles. They contain the New Testament, the Old Testament, and even have apocryphal books mixed in. (They are called Sinaiticus, Vaticanus, and Alexandrinus.) The men who wrote them thought they could make God's words "better." So they added some *words*, *phrases*, and even whole *books*. And they also took away other words, whole verses and even some entire chapters!
>
> But that is not all. They could not agree with each other on what should be put into their

> Bibles. So Alexandrian manuscripts don't even
> agree with each other![9]

Throughout history, the Received Texts were the Greek and Hebrew texts that God's people always recognized to be the true representation of God's inspired words. It wasn't until the 1800s that orthodox Christians succumbed to the plot to undermine and dethrone the Received Texts.

In 1831, Lachmann produced a Greek New Testament based upon the corrupt Vaticanus manuscript. Constantin Tishendorf, the man who discovered the corrupt Sinaiticus manuscript in a wastepaper basket, produced a series of Greek texts in 1841-1869 of which the latter editions were based heavily upon Sinaiticus.

Others who produced editions of the Greek New Testament based on the Alexandrian manuscripts (mainly Vaticanus and Sinaiticus) were Alford (1849), Wordsworth (1856), and Tragelles (1857).

These corrupt Alexandrian-based Greek texts became known as the Critical Texts. In 1881, the Critical Texts were made popular through the edition of the Greek New Testament produced by Brooke Foss Westcott and Fenton J. A. Hort. The Westcott and Hort text was secretly and deceptively smuggled into the revision of the English Bible (known as the 1881 Revised Version), replacing the Textus Receptus as the New Testament basis.

Today these Critical Texts are represented in the works of Eberhard Nestle, Kurt Aland, and the United Bible Society.

---

9) Gary Miller, *Why the King James Bible is the Perfect Word of God*, pp. 39-40.

REVISION WORK
IN THE 1800s

The influence of the developing Critical Text movement began making its mark on the Spanish Bible even before Westcott and Hort's era.

In 1862, Dr. Lorenzo Lucena, a professor at Oxford University, revised the Valera. Fortunately, he removed the Apocrypha, which had been between the Old and New Testaments of the Valera Bible. Unfortunately, his revision of the rest of the text introduced more corruptions based upon the Critical Texts.

According to Dr. Rex Cobb's chart, mentioned earlier, this 1862 revision departed from the Textus Receptus 122 times, which is double the number of departures from the Textus Receptus in the 1602 Valera.

Prior to Dr. Lucena's revision, there were other revisions. The Glasgow Bible Society (GBS) published a revision in 1831, which was reprinted by the American Bible Society (ABS) in 1845 and again by the GBS in 1849.

The British and Foreign Bible Society published their own revision in 1858. Many other revisions were also done throughout the 1800s.

In 1865 the ABS published yet another major revision. The two men called upon for this task were Angel Herreros de Mora and H. B. Pratt.

Mora, a Spaniard, was a former Catholic priest who later served in the Episcopal church.[10] Pratt was an American

---

10) Project Canterbury, Report of the Spanish Evangelical Church at Lisbon 1868-1872. www.anglicanhistory.org/europe/lisbon_spanish1872.html

Presbyterian missionary in Bogota, Columbia. They started their work in 1861 and finished in 1865.

This revision was an improvement since Mora and Pratt brought the Valera Bible closer to the Received Texts. Dr. Cobb found only 28 departures from the Textus Receptus. Though this revision was a step forward in purifying the Valera Bible, issues still remained.

As Carlos Donate points out:

> Many verses of the New Testament were revised following the Received Text and the Authorized Version, although others that should have been revised remained the same like before, corrupt or not very well translated.[11]

Following are some problems in the 1865 from a chart by Michael Lemma, veteran missionary in Mexico and one of Dr. Gómez's collaborators:

1. Leviticus 16:8, 10, 26 – has the Hebrew transliteration *Azazel.* (Note: the RVG is the only Spanish Bible that translates the word "scapegoat.")

2. Numbers 31:34, 39 says "seventy and one" instead of "sixty and one."

3. Judges 3:7 says that God forgot Israel instead of Israel forgetting God, which is totally opposite.

4. 2 Samuel 22:6 says "the cords of the sepulcher girded me" instead of "The sorrows of hell compassed me about."

5. 2 Kings 2:9 says "two parts of thy spirit" instead of "double portion of thy spirit."

---

11) Carlos Donate, The Antigua Valera Bible.

6. Psalm 18:5, Proverbs 7:27 say "sepulcher" instead of "hell."

7. Psalm 104:4 – says "his ministers to the flaming fire" instead of "his ministers a flaming fire."

8. Proverbs 27:20 says the "grave" is never full instead of "hell."

9. Daniel 7:13 says "a Son of man" instead of "the Son of man."

10. Hosea 4:12 says "their gods" instead of "their God."

11. Habakkuk 2:5 says "ossuary" (*osario*) instead of "hell." An ossuary is a place to keep dead men's bones.

12. Mark 15:3* "but he answered nothing" is omitted.

13. Matthew 24:2*; Luke 9:43*, Romans 15:17; Philippians 3:12; 2 Timothy 3:12 "Jesus" is omitted.

14. Luke 13:35* "verily" is omitted.

15. John 14:28 says "the Father" instead of "my Father" (Textus Receptus says πατηρ μου, "Father of me").

16. Acts 5:23 "without" is omitted.

17. Acts 8:16*, Acts 22:16* – "the Lord" is omitted.

18. Titus 2:7* "sincerity" is omitted.

19. 2 Peter 2:4* says "tartarus" (Spanish *tartaro*) instead of "hell." (Note: Verses with an asterisk * were corrected in a revised edition of the 1865 Valera.)

Unfortunately, the President of a small Bible society in Florida that is responsible for the promotion and circulation of this revised 1865 text stated publicly that his society recently voted to reject these good changes. They plan to reprint the 1865 with all the omissions and issues mentioned above as well as many more not mentioned here.)

THE 1909 ANTIGUA

Prior to 1909, the British and Foreign Bible Society attempted several revisions of the Reina-Valera Bible. But in 1909, they published another major revision (in conjunction with the ABS.) Translators representing several Latin American countries had been commissioned for this work.

None were as successful as this one, which became affectionately known as the Antigua Version. It quickly became the standard Spanish Bible among Fundamentalists throughout Latin America.

Unfortunately, Critical Texts were incorporated in this revision. (Examples of corruptions are listed later.)

THE 1960
REINA-VALERA BIBLE

In the mid 1900s, the American Bible Society undertook another major Spanish Bible revision, which was published in 1960. A 1971 report from the coordinator of this revision states:

> Actually, by means of a succession of minor revisions, of which the 1909 was the latest and most extensive, more than 100,000 changes of spelling, orthography, and punctuation were introduced and well over 60,000 changes of wording.[12]

The RV 1960 has since replaced the 1909 as the most popular and most used edition of the Spanish Bible among Hispanic Fundamentalists.

---

12) Eugene Nida, Reina-Valera Spanish Revision of 1960, *The Bible Translator,* p. 107.

Many have even switched from the 1909 Antigua to the 1960 revision despite the fact that the groundwork for Fundamentalism in Latin American countries was laid through the 1909 edition.

ENTER EUGENE NIDA

The man the ABS appointed to head up this project was Eugene Nida, who was the Executive Secretary of the American Bible Society at the time. Perhaps no man of the 20th century has influenced the work of Bible translation based on the Alexandrian Critical Texts more than Nida.

In the preface of the UBS Greek New Testament, Eugene Nida is credited as being the one who "initiated, organized, and administered" the making of the UBS's first edition of the Alexandrian-based critical Greek New Testament which was published in 1966.[13]

The second edition of this same text became the Greek basis for the New International Version (NIV).

The Eugene Nida Institute for Biblical Scholarship claims that a milestone in his life was when he became a:

> Key figure in forging UBS/Vatican agreement
> to undertake hundreds of interconfessional
> Bible translation projects worldwide, using
> functional equivalence principles.[14]

It is no secret that Eugene Nida is the man responsible for influencing the alliance between the United Bible Societies

---

13) UBS Greek New Testament, 1966, Preface p. vi.
14) From a Brief Biography of Eugene Nida at:
www.nidainstitute.org/vsItemDisplay.dsp&objectID=0920A817-28AA-
4D6F-9B9F70012FE3A462&method=display

(UBS) and the Vatican of Rome. The American Bible Society (ABS) is now the American chapter of the UBS.

Thanks to Nida's efforts, the UBS is now an official member of the ecumenical World Council of Churches.[15]

Due to copyright laws, every time someone purchases a Reina-Valera 1960, a percentage goes directly to the UBS. Preachers who support the RV 1960 downplay this fact by claiming that the percentage is so small it is insignificant.

However, considering the popularity the Reina-Valera 1960 has enjoyed for the many years since its inception, it is a wonder that Fundamentalists are not unanimously outraged that a percentage of their finances, regardless of the amount, is going to support a liberal, modernist, pro-Catholic, ecumenical organization.

The 1960 Reina-Valera Bible is not the only Spanish Bible project overseen by Nida. He also oversaw the translation committee that produced the Spanish version of Today's English Version, also known as the Good News for Modern Man. This was an ecumenical effort. Nida said of this Bible translation committee, which consisted of both Catholics and Protestants:

> It was a great experience to see how Latin American Roman Catholics and Protestants could work together so creatively. Perhaps the most gratifying aspect of this program was to see how the Roman Catholic participants were even more sensitive to possible adverse reac-

---

15) www.oikoumene.org

tions of Protestants than even the Protestant members of the team had been.[16]

This man who headed up the revision of the RV 1960 considered it "gratifying" to see Catholics and Protestants working together successfully.

Supporters of the RV 1960 make much of the fact that Nida did not participate in voting matters, a privilege exercised only by the members of the revision committee. However, he did not need voting privileges to influence the RV 1960 since he not only chose the men for the committee but also organized the procedures and supervised the work.[17]

NIDA'S VIEW OF TRANSLATING

In a *Christianity Today* magazine interview, Nida explained his standard procedure in dealing with translation committees:

> When we bring together a group of folks who want to be translators, it takes a month to get them willing to make sense intellectually. It takes another two weeks to make them willing to do it emotionally. They can accept it intellectually but not emotionally because they've grown up worshiping words more than worshiping God.
>
> We can't have conferences for new translators in less than six weeks because of this psychological hurdle. Otherwise, within a year's time they

---

16) Eugene Nida, *Fascinated by Languages,* p. 136.
17) Eugene Nida, Reina-Valera Spanish Revision of 1960, *The Bible Translator,* pp. 115-116. Note: This article by Nida lays out the details of how involved he was with the Revision Committee.

> will be producing literal translations because
> it's so much easier to do it word-for-word.
>
> Bible translators often think they must aim
> at almost exact verbal correspondence to the
> original in order to make sense. Many of them
> insist there must be consistency of words. But
> consistency in principal words is misleading
> because words have a variety of meanings
> depending on context.
>
> So a translator can be consistently wrong as
> well as consistently right. This "word wor-
> ship" helps people to have confidence, but
> they don't understand the text. And as long
> as they worship words, instead of worshiping
> God as revealed in Jesus Christ, they feel safe.[18]

The method of translating that Nida is advocating here is known as Dynamic Equivalence (DE). It is sometimes also known as Functional Equivalence. It places an emphasis on translating the message, ideas, or concepts behind the words rather than translating the actual preserved words of God themselves.

Nida did not invent DE, but he is the one credited with popularizing this translating method. Thus, Eugene Nida is known as "the father of dynamic equivalency."

Contrast the complaints of Nida against the translating of the actual words of God, a practice which he refers to as "word worship," to the following verses of scriptures:

---

18) From an interview with *Christianity Today*: www.christianitytoday.com/ct/2002/october7/2.46.html?start=1

> Have not I written to thee excellent things in
> counsels and knowledge, That I might make
> thee know the certainty of the words of truth;
> that thou mightest answer the words of truth
> to them that send unto thee?[19]
>
> Heaven and earth shall pass away, but my words
> shall not pass away.[20]
>
> The words of the LORD are pure words: as
> silver tried in a furnace of earth, purified seven
> times. Thou shalt keep them, O LORD, thou
> shalt preserve them from this generation for
> ever.[21]

Nowhere in the Bible does God promise to preserve the
message, concept, idea, principle, or philosophy behind the
words. God clearly promises to preserve His *words*!

Therefore, the Bible translator's job is to translate the
words, not his opinion about the message behind the words.
Once God's words are preserved through accurate and faithful
translating, the message will also be preserved.

Concerning this modernistic philosophy of translating,
Dr. Jack Moorman, an avid defender of the KJV, says:

> Virtually all recent translations and the Bible
> Societies' work generally has been to a large
> extent influenced by Dynamic Equivalence.
> It has made Eugene Nida the most influential
> person in the field. The theory is grounded

---

19) Proverbs 22:20-21.
20) Matthew 24:35.
21) Psalm 12:6-7.

in theological liberalism. It strips the Bible of its doctrinal content. It dishonours God by implying He is unable to speak absolutely to all generations and cultures. And to quote the verdict that a literary critic gave the New International Version, it makes the Bible "formica flat.[22]

The theological liberalism that Dr. Moorman is referring to is the modernistic idea known as *Conceptual Inspiration*. It is a diabolical heresy and is a view held by modernists and liberals. This idea is in opposition to the fundamental of the faith known as Verbal Inspiration of the scriptures.

Verbal Inspiration is the belief that God inspired the very words of the scriptures ("Every word of God is pure...[23]").

Conceptual Inspiration is the view that God did not inspire the words, but the message, ideas, thoughts, philosophies, or concepts behind the words. This view has absolutely no scriptural support. The translating practice that is consistent with this heretical view is Nida's Dynamic Equivalence method.

To stray from translating the words to translating the message behind the words violates the Bible's clear commands against altering, subtracting, or adding to God's words.[24]

As can be seen in Nida's *Christianity Today* interview, Nida saw to it that the translating committees he was involved with implemented his philosophies of Bible translation. There is

22) www.deanburgonsociety.org/idx_foreign_bible_versions.htm
23) Proverbs 30:5.
24) Deuteronomy 4:2, Proverbs 30:6, and Revelation 22:19.

no reason to believe that the committee he coordinated to revise the Spanish Bible was any different.

Nida's influence on the RV 1960 revision committee is obvious. One staunch supporter of the RV 1960 declares:

> In the Spanish Bibles through 1909 there was an intention to render the Hebrew text literally, while beginning with the 1960 revision it was decided to convey the actual meaning and not the actual word.[25]

THE RV 1960 AND THE CRITICAL TEXTS

Nida's influence on the 1960 revision committee is plainly seen by the incorporation of the Alexandrian Critical Texts. Eugene Nida openly admits that the departures from the Textus Receptus and the incorporation of the Critical Texts were deliberate:

> Nevertheless in some instances where a critical text is so much preferred over the traditional Textus Receptus the committee did make some slight changes, particularity if such changes were not in well-known verses...[26]

Dr. Jose Flores, who was the President of the Spanish Bible Society and a consultant to the RV 1960 revision committee, reveals not just the incorporation of Critical Texts, but Critical Text-based *English* translations as well.

He adds:

25) Calvin George, *The Battle for the Spanish Bible*, pp. 20-21.
26) The Bible Translator, Vol. 12, No. 3, 1961, p. 113.

One principle added to the first list of the RV 1960 revision committee was that wherever the RV (1909) Version has departed from the Textus Receptus to follow a better text we did not return to the Receptus. Point 12 of the working principles states: in cases where there is a doubt over the correct translation of the original, we consulted preferentially The English Revised Version of 1885, The American Standard Version of 1901, The Revised Standard Version of 1946, and the International Critical Commentary.[27]

Even some of the most outspoken supporters of the RV 1960 have admitted to the presence of Critical Texts in this revision. One such author admits:

There are a few translations in the 1909 and 1960 that may not be able to be traced to differences in TR (Textus Receptus) editions or semantics. A few departures come from a critical text.[28]

Furthermore, this same author confesses:

I believe Westcott and Hort texts can be consulted in the process of translating (such was the case in the Reina-Valera 1909 and 1960); however, it must not form the basis for a translation.[29]

27) Dr. Jose Flores, *El Texto Del Nuevo Testamento,* CLIE 1977, p. 323.
28) Calvin George, *The Battle for the Spanish Bible*, p. 42.
29) Ibid. p. 115.

We will see that in the RV 1960 the Critical Texts served as the basis for more than just a few important doctrinal passages.

CORRUPTION IN THE
RV 1909 AND 1960

Tim Urling, a veteran missionary in Mexico, wrote an article entitled *38 Reasons Why I Cannot Use the 1960 Reina-Valera*.[30] In it, he provides 38 examples of corruption in the RV 1960. Twenty of those errors also exist in the RV 1909 Antigua. Each error that is also found in the 1909 is marked with an asterisk (*):

1. The RV 1960 says man became a living "being" instead of a living "soul" in Genesis 2:7.

2. The 1960 contains a false and contradictory statement about who killed Goliath in 2 Samuel 21:19.*

3. The phrase "and increased the joy" in Isaiah 9:3 is the exact opposite of the King James and previous Spanish Bibles.

4. In Daniel 3:25 Nebuchadnezzar declares that the form of the fourth man he saw in the fire was like "a son of the gods."*

5. In Matthew chapter one, the word "begat" is omitted 22 times in violation of Revelation 22:19.

6. In Matthew 5:22 the words "without a cause" are omitted, making Christ a sinner when he got angry.

7. Matthew 6:1 changes the word "alms" to "justice."*

---

30) Visit Tim Urling's website to see this article in its entirety:
www.2everycreature.citymax.com/newsletters/newsletter/5001767/45126.htm

8. "Draweth nigh to me with their mouths" has been removed from Matthew 15:8.*

9. "yet they found none" is left out of Matthew 26:60.*

10. In Mark 1:2 "in the prophets" was changed to "in Isaiah the prophet."*

11. "to repentance" was omitted from Mark 2:17.*

12. In Mark 11:10 the words "in the name of our Lord" have been left out.*

13. Mark 15:39 is changed from "Truly this man was the Son of God" to "a Son of God."

14. Luke 2:22 talks about the days of "their" (Mary and Jesus) cleansing. According to the Old Testament law Jesus did not need to be purified.

15. The words "in spirit" are omitted in Luke 2:40.*

16. The word "hell" is changed to *Hades* in Luke 16:23 and other verses. The word "hell" appears 54 times in the KJV but only 13 times in the Reina-Valera 1960 (and only 32 times in the RV 1909).

17. The repentant thief does not recognize Jesus as "Lord" in Luke 23:42.*

18. In John 6:22 the words "save that one whereinto his disciples were entered" were not included.*

19. John 12:47 changes "believe" to "keep."

20. In Acts 6:8, "faith" has been changed to "grace."*

21. "of the Lord" was left out when Stephen described the angel of the burning bush incident in Acts 7:30.*

22. "and the Lord said" was omitted in Acts 9:5.*

23. In Acts 15:18, "Known unto God are all his works" has been completely changed to, "Says the Lord, make known all of this."

24. In Acts 18:5 "Paul was pressed in the spirit" was changed to "Paul was completely surrendered to the preaching of the word."*

25. Romans 1:16 leaves out the words "of Christ" when speaking "of the gospel of Christ."*

26. Romans 10:9 says "if you confess with your mouth that Jesus is the Lord..." instead of "if thou shalt confess with thy mouth the Lord Jesus..." Biblical salvation is not just saying "Jesus is the Lord."

27. The words "believed," "unbelief," and "not believed" were changed to "disobedient" and "disobedience" in Romans 11:30-32.

28. 1 Corinthians 7:3 changes the word "conjugal" to "benevolence."

29. 1 Corinthians 7:5 leaves out "fasting" when talking about prayer and fasting.*

30. The words "by Jesus Christ" were not included in Ephesians 3:9.*

31. In 1 Thessalonians 4:4 the translators changed the word "vessel" to "wife."

32. "But unto the Son" was changed to "but of the Son" in Hebrews 1:8.

33. 1 Peter 2:2 is changed to read "that by it you'll grow for salvation." (or to be saved, or in order to be saved). It also makes no mention of the "word."*

34. Jude 22 was changed from saying correctly, "And of some have compassion, making a difference…" to "to some that doubt, convince."

35. Revelation 14:1 adds "His name and," making the 144,000 *also* have the Lamb's name, along with His Father's name, written in their foreheads. The KJV and Textus Receptus only mention them having the name of the Father.

36. Revelation 18:20 adds a comma between *santos* and *apóstoles*, changing one group, "holy apostles," into two groups, "saints" and "apostles."*

37. In Revelation 22:6 "the Lord God of the holy prophets…" was changed to "the God of the spirits of the prophets…"

38. Revelation 22:14 was changed from "Blessed are they that do his commandments" to "Blessed are those that wash their clothes (or robes)."

Many other examples could be provided but these should be enough to demonstrate the seriousness of the Critical Text errors that exist in revisions of the Spanish Bible.

For many years Spanish-speaking Bible-believing Christians have dreamed of and prayed for a Spanish Bible that is 100% free of Alexandrian corruption, and conforms to the Received Texts and is equivalent to the KJV, yet keeps the majestic beauty of the Reina-Valera Bible's Castilian Spanish.

By the grace of God, many believe that dream has finally come true and those prayers have been answered through the Reina-Valera Gómez 2010.

CHAPTER 4

Principles of the Reina-Valera Gómez Revision

But he answered and said, It is written, Man
shall not live by bread alone, but by every word
that proceedeth out of the mouth of God.[31]

Now we come to the Reina-Valera Gómez Bible. This
author spent countless hours corresponding with Dr. Gómez
– over the phone, by email and instant messenger, and in
person – to learn about the motives, mindset, and methods
behind RVG revision project.

In these next two chapters, we will see the factors that
contributed to the making of the RVG Bible as conveyed
by Dr. Gómez and his collaborators.

---

31) Matthew 4:4.

Many Christians do not understand why and when Bible revision becomes necessary. Cipriano de Valera's twenty year effort to purify the text that Casiodoro de Reina translated stemmed from a sincere and fervent desire for his people to have access to the most accurate translation of God's pure words as possible.

This was the desire of Dr. Gómez and his collaborators as well. Over the years, Bible-believing Fundamentalists have pinpointed the Alexandrian corruptions introduced in the Spanish Bible.

After many years of collecting information on this subject, and through much prayer and counseling, beginning in the year 2000, Dr. Gómez took upon himself, as he puts it, "with fear and trembling" (Isaiah 66:2), the task of purifying the Reina-Valera text.

In 2004, after the publishing of the first edition of the Reina-Valera Gómez Bible, Dr. Gómez wrote an article entitled *The Spanish Bible Issue* to briefly explain his work of revising the Spanish Bible.

In this article, he laid out three major principles that guided him and his collaborators in their work:

1. First and foremost 100% loyalty to the pure texts, Textus Receptus for the New Testament, and the Masoretic Text for the Old Testament.

2. Apply all the beauty of our Spanish language with all its romanticism, prose, and elegance.

3. Apply all the beauty and accuracy of the King James Bible that can be applied to our language, without butchering, distorting, or destroying our language.

THE THEOLOGICAL PREMISE

Bible-believing Fundamentalists have always been diametrically opposed to the Alexandrian Critical Texts, and therefore have not hesitated to call for the revision of any foreign translation that has been corrupted.

We also share this stand because of our conviction in what the Lord said in Matthew 4:4. It was the Lord Himself who declared the necessity of *every word of God* for our spiritual well-being. Therefore we demand nothing less than a Bible with *every word of God* accurately translated.

This cannot be accomplished through the incorporation of and reliance upon corrupt Critical Texts where they contradict the pure readings of the Textus Receptus.

Therefore, for a Bible to be completely accurate, it must be completely based on and in conformity to the right texts without any insertions of the corrupt texts.

It must be also driven by the proper translating philosophy. Dr. Gómez's philosophy of Bible translating is consistent with this theological premise. As we touched on earlier, Fundamentalists believe in Verbal, Plenary Inspiration of the Scriptures. 'Verbal' means *word for word*. 'Plenary' means "full" or "complete."

Therefore Verbal, Plenary Inspiration deals with the inspiration of every word of God.

For a Bible to be a complete and faithful translation of God's words, every word that God inspired must be accurately translated into the receptor language (Matthew 4:4).

We also stand for Verbal, Plenary Preservation of the Scriptures. This is the belief in what the Scripture says about itself concerning Bible Preservation. God promised that *every word* He dictated to the holy apostles and prophets would be preserved from generation to generation.[32]

Dr. Gómez testifies that his goal in this revision has been to honor God, who magnifies His word above His very name (Psalm 138:2), by seeing to it that the very words that He inspired and preserved from generation to generation are accurately rendered in the Spanish language.

THE RIGHT PHILOSOPHY OF BIBLE TRANSLATING

The method of translating that emphasizes the translation of the words themselves rather than the meaning or message behind the words is known as Verbal, Plenary Translating. This is opposite to the method of translating promoted by Eugene Nida, Dynamic Equivalence (DE).

Verbal, Plenary Inspiration and Verbal, Plenary Preservation demands Verbal, Plenary Translating. It is the only translation philosophy that is consistent with what the Scriptures teach about the importance of "every word of God."

If God saw fit to preserve every word that He inspired, then it only stands to reason that, in order for a translation to be totally accurate, it must have *every* word of God faithfully translated.

We must not settle for a translation that has words omitted. As one preacher said, we should desire "the *whole* Bible, not a Bible full of *holes!*"

---

32) Psalm 12:6-7; 78:1-8, Isaiah 40:8; 59:21, Matthew 5:17-18; 24:35, 1 Peter 1:23-25.

The Verbal, Plenary method of translating is also known as Formal Equivalence or "word-for-word" translating. It has been around for a long time, and is the method the KJV translators used. One author stated in 1588:

> For it behooves a translation of Scripture not merely to take care that you do not corrupt the meaning but also as far as is at all possible not to depart a hand's breadth from the words since many things lie under the cover in the words of the Holy Spirit which are not immediately perceived but yet contains important instruction.[33]

We should not be satisfied with a Bible that is just 90% or 95% accurate. We should not even be satisfied with a Bible that is 99% accurate. The goal of every foreign Bible translator, or in this case —Bible reviser— should be a translation that is 100% correct since the Lord insisted out of his own mouth that *every* word of God is vital for our spiritual lives.

WORD-FOR-WORD TRANSLATING

I raise these points concerning translating philosophy to engage the concerns of some in regards to the difficulties that arose when trying to achieve exactness of wording from one language to another.

Dr. Gómez and his collaborators, being bilingual, were well aware of this challenge. But they still contended that a totally accurate Spanish translation of the Scriptures was possible by God's grace, despite the linguistic difficulties that

---

33) William Whitaker, *Disputations on the Holy Scripture*, p. 165.

existed. This is why it is very important for Bible translators and revisers to be Spirit-led men of God, for as Jesus said:

> With men this is impossible; but with God
> all things are possible.[34]

Many fail to understand that Verbal, Plenary Translating is not a demand for a word-for-word equivalent in every single instance. It is a demand for a "word-for-word" equivalent *wherever it is possible.*

Wherever an exact verbal equivalent is not possible, the translator's job is to seek God's direction in choosing a word (or words) that most accurately represents the word or words in the source language.

There are always exceptions to the rule, especially in regards to idiomatic expressions. Such exceptions are understandable, but they only prove the rule.

Keep in mind that most words in every language have a literal equivalent in another language. In each case the literal word-for-word equivalent should be used as long as it makes sense in the receptor language.

Dr. H. D. Williams, the Vice President of the Dean Burgon Society, and a strong supporter of the RVG Bible, wrote a book on "word-for-word" translating entitled *Word-For-Word Translating of the Received Texts: Verbal Plenary Translating.*[35]

Through his practice in the medical field, of which he is now retired, he has experience in translating from Latin

---

34) Matthew 19:26.
35) Available through the Dean Burgon Society bookstore, or online at: www.amazon.com/Word-Translating-Received-Verbal-Plenary/dp/1568480563

to English. Dr. Williams says:

> DE theorists mistakenly think that word-for-word translating is only one word for one word and only one class of words (nouns, verbs, pronouns, etc.) for one class of words. Although the primary attempt should be one word for one word or one class for one class, the syntax of language determines the final disposition of translating.
>
> Nothing could be further from the truth than the accusation by modern language theorists that word-for-word translating is rigid. Rather, it is militancy for accurate and faithful translation of His words! Literal word-for-word translating is translating words in the source language for words in the receptor-language so far as the syntax of the receptor-language will allow.
>
> No one would deny the difficulty that often occurs, but the primary aim of translators is for His glory though faithful preservation of His glorious Words (Isaiah 42:8) in any language.[36]

Understanding these things will help the Christian to understand why there are times in the KJV and RVG that are not exactly identical. Some have charged that the instances in the RVG that do not exactly mirror the wording of the KJV are in error, or in disagreement with the KJV, or an

---

36) Dr. H.D. Williams, *Word-For-Word Translating of the Received Texts: Verbal Plenary Translating*, p. 4.

inferior translation of the Received Texts.

This is not so. On the contrary, one of Dr. Gómez's collaborators (Carlos Donate) explains:

> Despite what some may say to the contrary, we have studied all options out there and like yourselves, prayerfully decided that the RVG is indeed the best alternative as far a pure Spanish Bible.
>
> Having been a part of another well known project, I myself took the idea of comparing and checking out in detail what my best option was, and praise God, the RVG is the Bible that the Holy Spirit led me to adopt.
>
> We have concluded that there is absolutely no textual error in the RVG—none! What others think are textual departures are actually not departures from the Received Text at all, but rather alternate, polysemic, or variants of formal equivalence readings and/or translational alternates.
>
> Dr. Gómez did some changes in the receptor language (Spanish) to improve upon the language without affecting the underlying Hebrew and Greek text. He did so with the consent of many of us native Spanish-speaking pastors and missionaries.[37]

The point is that although a word-for-word equivalent

---

37) Email correspondence between Carlos Donate and Chick Publications, on file.

and exactness should be the primary goal and focus, instances in the translation where such was not possible do not necessarily represent a disagreement with the Textus Receptus or the KJV.

Many times there is a pool of words or phrases that can be used, all of which could be accurate. The translator's job is to choose the word or words that (A) are the most accurate in its agreement with the KJV and traditional texts and (B) also makes the most sense in the receptor language.

REMAINING TRUE TO OUR HERITAGE

A misconception is that the goal of Dr. Gómez was to produce a KJV in Spanish. This is not so. He has publicly, and on numerous occasions, made it clear that his firm conviction is that God gave the Spanish-speaking world the Reina-Valera Bible, the greatest literary work in the history of the Spanish language.

This traditional form of the Bible has been and should continue to be the standard format for the Spanish-speaking people. God has placed his stamp of approval upon it. This is evidenced by its fruit, and the loyalty of Hispanic Bible-believers that it has enjoyed in the history of both Hispanic Fundamentalism and Protestantism.

The Reina-Valera Bible is part of our heritage. To try and replace it would be to dishonor what God has done for the Spanish-speaking world.

Others have tried to replace the Reina-Valera in the past by starting a whole new Spanish translation of either the KJV or one of the other ancient Spanish Bibles (such as Enzina's New Testament). Despite how noble their intentions may have been, there is a good reason why their efforts were not successful.

We did not believe that replacing the form of the Reina-Valera was the answer. Dr. Gómez's effort was *revision* not *replacement*. Thus, the Reina-Valera Gómez is not a Spanish carbon copy of the English KJV but rather a version of the Reina-Valera that is equivalent to the KJV, yet true to its root form.

In fact, many of the changes that were made were simply readings that already existed over four hundred years ago in the original 1602 Valera. Thus, in many places the RVG has actually returned to its original form as rendered over four hundred years ago.

For example, in Luke 23:42 the KJV says:

> And he said unto Jesus, Lord, remember me when thou comest into thy kingdom.

The RV 1909 and 1960 both omit the word "Lord" *(Señor)*. Yet that word "Lord" was included in this verse in the original 1602 Valera just like it is rendered in the KJV.

Dr. Gómez and his collaborators reinserted the word "Lord" back to its rightful place in Luke 23:42 in the RVG, thus returning to its original rendering.

Another example is in Mark 1:2. The KJV says:

> As it is written in the prophets, Behold, I send my messenger before thy face, which shall prepare thy way before thee.

The RV 1909 and 1960 change "written in the prophets" to "written in Isaiah the prophet…" (The NIV, ASV, RSV, and most other Alexandrian-based Bibles in English do the same thing). This is a gross error because both quotes in Mark 1:2-3 are *not* from the prophet Isaiah. One does quote Isaiah (40:3) but the other quotes Malachi (3:1).

So the KJV is correct in saying "in the prophets." The original 1602 is also correct for it also says "in the prophets."

Dr. Gómez and his collaborators changed Mark 1:2 to read "in the prophets" (*en los profetas*) returning to its original wording as in the 1602 Valera and consequently matching the KJV and Textus Receptus.

Many other verses in the RVG have also been returned to their original reading as they stood in the 1602 Valera. These renderings were correct to begin with. But according to Eugene Nida, they were changed because the 1960 revision committee considered them to be

> …instances where a critical text is so much preferred over the traditional Textus Receptus…[38]

BY SPANISH SPEAKERS- FOR SPANISH SPEAKERS

It is important for our good American brethren to understand that this Bible is first and foremost for the Spanish-speaking natives in Spanish-speaking countries.

This may seem obvious but it needs to be emphasized because some well-meaning American brethren who speak Spanish may disagree with some of Dr. Gómez's word choices.

---

38) The Bible Translator, Vol. 12, No. 3, 1961, p. 113.

But they fail to understand that there is a difference between approaching the Spanish text from a Hispanic mindset and an American English-speaking mindset.

For example, the translation of idioms requires more than just a conversational fluency. It requires an understanding of the receptor language at a level that usually only a native who grew up with that language possesses.

Many times it is impossible to translate idiomatic expressions in a literal word-for-word fashion. In these cases an exception must be made. Those who study the translating methods of the KJV translators will see that they also made exceptions when dealing with idiomatic expressions.

Some of our well-meaning American brethren fail to realize that many Hispanic natives in Spanish-speaking countries, who speak no English, will not understand a literal word-for-word translation of idiomatic expressions.

So understanding the people and their language from a native's viewpoint (as many of our collaborators, including its chief editor, are natives), they translated certain expressions in a way that (1) native Hispanics in any Spanish-speaking country can understand but (2) in no way conflicts with the Received Texts nor the KJV.

AN INTERNATIONAL ENDEAVOR

This is why it has been important for Dr. Gómez to have the collaboration of not just one Spanish-speaking country but many. This has not been solely a Mexican project. This surely has not been an American project. This has been a world-wide endeavor.

Dr. Gómez and his collaborators were fully aware of the various nuances that exist in different Spanish-speaking countries. Therefore they included the valuable input of those representing such countries as Spain, Peru, Guatemala, Chile, Argentina, Costa Rica, Paraguay, Belize, Cuba, Ecuador, and of course all over Mexico.

Dr. Gómez personally travelled to some of these countries and spoke face-to-face with nationals around the world who offered good advice concerning the different nuances of their language. Over the years he accumulated the input of well over 200 brethren around the world with concerns and suggestions for certain renderings in the RVG text.

This is not to say that they did not include the input of American brethren who are fluent in Spanish and have a true burden and love for the Hispanic people. As will be seen in chapter 5, they surely did. But the final word choices came from a Hispanic mindset with the Hispanic native in mind.

THE FOUNDATION

Let it be understood that the foundational basis for this revision was indeed the Received Texts. Dr. Gómez believes that the traditional Received Texts are the true representation of the original autographs, preserved from generation to generation.

As already mentioned, the primary principle in this revision was:

> First and foremost 100% loyalty to the pure texts, Textus Receptus for the New Testament, and the Masoretic Text for the Old Testament.

The history of Bible manuscripts demonstrates that the text of the Traditional Text (or Received Text) family can be traced all the way back to the Apostolic age (in the Italic version and Syrian Peshitta).

In other words, there is an unbroken chain of manuscript evidence from the Apostolic age to today supporting the text that underlies the KJV.

Dr. D. A. Waite demonstrates this evidence on pages 44-48 of his book *Defending the King James Bible* under the heading "The Thirty-Seven Historical Evidences Supporting the Textus Receptus."

This evidence demonstrates the type of text that represents the fulfillment of God's promises to preserve his pure words from generation to generation.

Every change that was implemented to create the RVG was thoroughly examined as to its accuracy with the Received Texts in Hebrew and in Greek.

Men with a proficiency in the original languages collaborated on this project to ensure accuracy with the Received Texts.

One such individual is Dr. D. A. Waite, the President and Founder of the Dean Burgon Society. Dr. Waite has been the primary consultant concerning the original languages.

This man has experience in teaching Greek and Hebrew since 1945. Most so-called "scholars" today could not hold a candle to the long list of linguistic credentials Dr. Waite possesses (which will be given later).

Another collaborator worth noting is Dr. Rex Cobb, an experienced Bible translator who also served as a church planting missionary in Mexico for many years. He now serves as the director of the Baptist Bible Translators Institute in Bowie, Texas, where missionaries are trained in the original languages and advanced linguistics for the purpose of translating the scriptures into languages and dialects around the world. His input was greatly valued.

Many others with training in the original languages, who uphold the Received Texts over the Critical Texts, have been involved in this project in many different ways, some more than others. But all have been extremely helpful, perhaps even more than they realize.

However, although the Received Texts served as the foundation for this revision, the collation went further than just the original languages. It has been customary for all Bible translators throughout history to heavily consult other accurate Textus Receptus-based translations.

This work has been no different. Dr. Gómez unashamedly admits that he also implemented the King James Bible. With the KJV, translators possess a sure standard of accuracy to guide them in their work every step of the way.

THE STANDARD

Dr. Gómez's position is:

> In the King James Bible we have the preservation of the inspired, perfect, infallible, inerrant Word of God.

This author shares the same position. The KJV contains no errors whatsoever and is a finished and purified text that can never be improved upon.

Since the KJV perfectly preserves in English for us the very words that God inspired in the original autographs, it is the best standard to follow to ensure accuracy with the preserved original language texts.

Dr. Gómez has been criticized by those who support the RV 1960 for this statement made in an address to the Dean Burgon Society in Chicago concerning his revision work:

> But the Standard to follow has to be the King James. This I say in public and I am not ashamed of this: 100%.

Those who object to using the KJV as the standard for revision of the Spanish Bible forget that the Spanish versions they advocate were also revised with English Bibles.

Remember the words of Dr. Jose Flores, who revealed that the 1960 revisers utilized "the English Revised Version of 1885, the American Standard Version of 1901, the Revised Standard Version of 1946, and the International Critical Commentary."

Just as the 1960 revisers did not hesitate to confess their reliance upon the Critical Texts and major English translations based upon them, we are just as bold in our reliance upon the KJV.

THE IMPORTANT ROLE OF THE KING JAMES VERSION

Some people allow that the KJV can be consulted as a secondary source but nothing more. Dr. Gómez disagrees (as does this author).

Though the foundational basis for any Bible translation

should be the Received Texts, the KJV should play a much greater role than just a secondary source, since it is more than just another accurate or faithful Protestant translation, though accurate and faithful it is. It is the very Word of God in English.

The KJV is the *crowning work* of the Received Texts.

A valid question that has been raised by those on both sides of the fence is in regards to which edition of the Textus Receptus should be considered the standard for foreign Bible translation or revision.

Should it be Beza's text? Or Stephanus? Erasmus? Colinaeus? Stunica? Elzivers?

Then, once you choose which text you will use, you must decide which edition of this text to use.

For example, Beza authored 10 different editions of his Greek New Testament. Which of his 10 editions would you choose?

Using the KJV as the standard eliminates this confusion, for the King's translators incorporated the best of all editions of the Received Texts. Perhaps Dr. Edward Hills explained it best:

> The texts of the several editions of the Textus Receptus were God-guided. They were set up under the leading of God's special providence. Hence the differences between them were kept down to a minimum... But what do we do in these few places in which the several editions of the Textus Receptus disagree with one another? Which text do we follow? The answer

to this question is easy. We are guided by the common faith.

Hence we favor that form of the Textus Receptus upon which, more than any other, God, working providentially, has placed the stamp of His approval, namely, the King James Version, or more precisely, the Greek text underlying the King James Version.

This text was published in 1881 by the Cambridge University Press under the editorship of Dr. Scrivener and there have been eight reprints, the latest being in 1949.

In 1976 also another edition of this text was published in London by the Trinitarian Bible Society. We ought to be grateful that in the providence of God the best form of the Textus Receptus is still available to believing Bible students.[39]

By incorporating the KJV in the work of foreign Bible translation, the translator is incorporating both its Greek and Hebrew basis and the textual decisions of the King's translators. This is the best form of the Received Texts to use for translation work.

It is important to note that not only did the KJV translators collate the Greek texts, they also compared prior English translations.

Also incorporated were the Complutensian and Antwerp

---

39) Dr. Edward Hills, *The King James Version Defended*, pg. 223.

Polyglots[40] and the Latin Bibles.[41] They also had the Italian Diodati, the French Olivetan, and Martin Luther's German Bible[42] available for their work of collation. As mentioned in the last chapter, they even had translations in Spanish at their disposal.

The point is that the underlying basis for the King James Bible was really not a singular text at all, but rather *a culmination of many texts* within the Traditional Text family that represented the overwhelming majority of manuscript evidence.

Therefore the KJV should be regarded as more than just another good and reliable translation. It is, as Dr. Hills puts it, "…an independent variety of the Textus Receptus." Dr. Hills explains:

> The translators that produced the KJV relied mainly, it seems, on the later editions of Beza's Greek New Testament, especially his 4th edition (1588-9). But also they frequently consulted the editions of Erasmus and Stephanus and the Complutensian Polyglot. According to Scrivener (1884), out of the 252 passages

---

40) Price, p. 271.

41) Hills, pp. 198-208. Note: Most readers assume "the Latin Vulgate" always refers to the corrupt Vulgate of Jerome. Not always. The Old Latin of the early Waldenses was also referred to as "the Latin Vulgate" for many years before Jerome produced his revision. (see J. J. Ray's *God Wrote Only One Bible,* p. 99). Also, both Erasmus and Beza translated their own Latin New Testaments. It is common knowledge that the KJV translators used them both. Therefore, it is highly probable that the Latin versions they collated may have been that of Erasmus and Beza and not just Jerome's. Miles Coverdale also edited his own version of the Latin Vulgate. Perhaps his was consulted as well.

42) D. O. Fuller, *Which Bible*, p. 212.

in which these sources differ sufficiently to affect the English rendering, the KJV agrees with Beza against Stephanus 113 times, with Stephanus against Beza 59 times, and 80 times with Erasmus, or the Complutensian, or the Latin Vulgate against Beza and Stephanus. Hence the King James Version ought to be regarded not merely as a translation of the Textus Receptus but also as an independent variety of the Textus Receptus.[43]

Although any of the Textus Receptus editions, from Erasmus to that of Scrivener's, is superior to any of the Critical Texts, each of these Textus Receptus Greek New Testaments was a revision. They were works *in transition* in efforts to improve upon the prior editions.

True Bible-believers believe that the KJV is the finality of the Textus Receptus and thus the final authority. It is the standard for accuracy. As Carlos Donate puts it:

The KJV stands alone, wholly perfect! It has been, and forever will be, the touchstone by which all faithful translations are to be judged. It is true to the TR (Textus Receptus) and MT (Masoretic Text), its underlying texts. Without apologies, and as a native Hispanic fluent in other languages besides my own, I vouch for the faithfulness of the KJV in total.[44]

When people reject the RVG on the basis of the involve-

---

43) Dr. Hills, *The King James Version Defended*, p. 220.
44) From an email correspondence.

ment of the KJV in the revision process, they do not realize that they are robbing themselves and others of using a Spanish Bible that represents the very best scholarship in the history of Bible translation. They also fail to realize that this is not an issue of a superior *language*, but an issue of superior *scholarship*.

In other words, KJV Bible-believers do not insist that foreign Bibles be revised using the KJV because the English language is superior to Spanish or any other language. We do not believe nor advocate that.

We insist that foreign Bible translators and revisers use the KJV as "the standard to follow" because the scholarship that produced it is superior to any other translation. And to apply the KJV is to apply its scholarship, its accuracy, and its purity.

In regards to the work of the King James translators, how can today's foreign Bible translator go wrong standing on the shoulders of these giants?

CHAPTER 5

The Making of the Reina-Valera Gómez Bible

Hope deferred maketh the heart sick: but when the desire cometh, it is a tree of life.[45]

Now that we have discussed the motives and principles that drove Dr. Gómez and his collaborators in their work of Bible revision, we will focus on how God worked to put it all together.

THE SPANISH BASE TEXT

The Spanish text that Dr. Gómez chose to revise is the 1909 Antigua version of the Reina-Valera. As mentioned in Chapter 1, this is the Bible that was used to bring him to salvation. It is also the Bible that he used for nearly thirty years in the ministry.

---

45) Proverbs 13:12.

To this day, Dr. Gómez testifies that this text is still near and dear to his heart. Other than sentimentality, the reasons Dr. Gómez and his collaborators went with this text are the following:

1. Despite the Critical Text readings that exist in the 1909 Antigua, by simple comparison it is a much purer text than the more popular RV 1960.

2. Though the 1909 Antigua is not identical to the original 1602 Valera, it manages to retain the beauty and grandeur of its root form. As even Eugene Nida recognizes, the 1909 retains the "flavor of the ages" that the Hispanic world has grown to love.[46] Considering the 60,000 changes of wording in the RV 1960, a Spanish Bible that is truer to its original form is preferred.

3. There are copyright issues that must be taken into consideration when choosing a Bible text to revise. When Chick Publications was investigating the RVG revision, they expressed their valid concerns of making sure the text was not in violation of any copyright laws.

Dr. Gómez solicited the help of Dr. D. A. Waite to confirm these matters to Chick Publications. This is what Dr. Waite wrote on December 3, 2007:

Dear Humberto,
I asked a lawyer who is the pastor of the Bible Presbyterian Church of Collingswood, New Jersey, about the 1909 and public domain. He

46) Eugene Nida, *The Bible Translator*, article "Reina-Valera Spanish Revision of 1960," p. 104.

is Dr. Christian Spencer who is a J.D. (Doctor of Jurisprudence); and also a pastor. He said that everything published before 1924 (I believe that was the date) is under PUBLIC DOMAIN. I asked if the Trinitarian Bible Society could put out a 1909 and copyright it. He said they could copyright their edition with certain notes and maps, etc, but under no circumstances can they or anyone else ever copyright the exact document that has been in public domain. The only thing they can copyright is their edition of the public domain material, not the public domain original material itself.

In Christ,

Pastor D. A. Waite

4. Considering the very significant place of the 1909 Antigua in the history of Hispanic Fundamentalism, there is still a strong loyalty to this beloved edition of the Spanish Bible.

Despite the popularity and availability of the RV 1960, many Hispanic preachers remained faithful to the 1909 Antigua edition both before *and after* the production of the new 1960 revision.

Dr. Thomas Holland, a Bible historian with a degree in Textual Criticism, states:

The 1960 edition was not overwhelmingly accepted when first produced. Deep within the hearts of the Spanish world there was a great devotion for the 1909 edition. Some rejected the changes made in the 1960 edition, calling for the Spanish-speaking Christian to remain faithful to the 1909 Valera.[47]

Eugene Nida himself supports Dr. Holland's statement with the following testimony:

> In fact, in some limited groups even the pastors were afraid to suggest the slightest changes in the text, for fear that they might seem to be tampering with the Word of God. On one occasion the very mention of "manuscripts" in a talk about the history of the Spanish Bible brought an expression of deep concern from one pastor, who arose and in an almost tearful plea, held out a battered copy of the Reina-Valera text (1909) and said, "But is not this the Word of God?[48]

Mexican pastor Ulises Velazquez testifies how these sentiments still exist today:

> In 1992 the first time someone told me about Christ they used the Reina-Valera 1909. I was living in Mexicali, B.C., Mexico. I worked for a company that rented commercial buildings since I had my title as a Bi-Lingual Administrative Assistant in the city of Durango.
>
> I was saved through this Bible and the first

47) Dr. Thomas Holland, article entitled "The Spanish Fountain."
48) "Reina-Valera Spanish Revision of 1960," *The Bible Translator* [New York: ABS, Vol. 13, No. 1, Jan. 1962], p. 108.

Bible that I bought was the 1909, a Bible that is close to my heart even today.

However, in the first Fundamental Independent Baptist church that I went to, they used the 1960, this was the most common Bible, and the one I used most to preach from.

In 1994, I went to a Missions Conference in Santa Catarina, N.L. and for the first time I witnessed something very unusual and new for me. I found brothers in Christ attacking and criticizing the version of the Bible that I used (the Reina-Valera 1960).

This greatly surprised me, and both bothered and frustrated me. They stood firmly behind the Antigua (Old Version) 1909. They defended it and refuted those that used any other 'modern' version.[49]

Carlos Donate adds:

In February of this year [2007], he [Dr. Humberto Gómez] was given the opportunity to speak before a congress of Hispanic fundamentalist leaders from USA, Mexico, Central and South America representing not just Baptists, but old time Methodists, Missionary Alliance, Bible Presbyterian, and Bible churches as well. This group has stood firmly for the 1909 Anti-

---

49) Ulises Velazquez, article "My Testimony About Using the Reina-Valera Gómez Bible."

gua ever since UBS began promoting Westcott
and Hort in the early 1950s.[50]

By using the 1909 Antigua as our Spanish base text,
those who have developed a sentimental attachment to this
Bible can still enjoy an edition of this same text, but one
that is free of Alexandrian corruption. Thus, the RVG revision is essentially the 1909 Antigua with all of the Critical
Texts removed.

The first book Dr. Gómez revised was the book of Romans,
which he finished in the year 2000. Before that year was
over, he completed the Pauline epistles.

In the beginning, he had little support in this massive
undertaking. In fact, the controversy over other projects that
likewise attempted to purify the Spanish Bible was becoming
more and more heated all the time. The sensitivity of this
issue made him very hesitant and cautious.

He tried to solicit the support and involvement of some
very well-respected and well-known Hispanic Fundamentalist
pastors. But their response was very unpleasant, to say the
least. One veteran missionary even warned Dr. Gómez that
if he went through with this plan to create a Reina-Valera
Gómez Bible that the majority of Hispanic Fundamentalist
pastors would blackball him.

Dr. Gómez has come to find out that the man was right.
But despite the cost, Dr. Gómez pressed on realizing that
a revision needed to be done regardless of what any man
may say or think.

---

50) Email correspondence.

DR. GÓMEZ
GOES FULL-TIME

Finally in 2001 Dr. Gómez decided to work full-time at revising the entire Spanish Bible.

In 2002 he completed the first draft of the New Testament. A printing ministry in southern Florida printed it that same year.

In 2004 he published the first edition of the entire Bible. Dr. Gómez's work was far from finished, as most of his attention was focused on correcting the textual errors in the New Testament. He did fix the most well-known issues in the Old Testament, such as Daniel 3:25, but a more thorough revision of the Old Testament was still needed.

Nevertheless, a friend named Dr. Thomas Gilmore, who is a representative of the Trinitarian Bible Society and is also involved in a revision of the Portuguese Bible, suggested that Dr. Gómez should go ahead and print his first edition even though it still had some flaws, and still needed a more thorough analysis of the Old Testament.

His idea was to get what he already had into the hands of the people so that it might generate interest as well as encourage the assistance of more collaborators from around the world.

THE FIRST EDITION
IS PRINTED

Other missionaries and pastors also encouraged him to print his first edition "as is" with the plan to continue his work with a more thorough examination and with the help of more collaborators.

As reluctant as Dr. Gómez was, he went through with the wishes of his brethren to print it despite its flaws. This move quickly drew the criticism of those who had been against his work since the beginning.

Eventually, though, it proved to be one of the best decisions that Dr. Gómez made in this project, considering the amount of support and collaboration that was generated as a result.

Dr. Gómez approached Bearing Precious Seed in Milford, Ohio about printing his text. The reaction of Dr. Stephen Zeinner, the director at the time, was very positive. His concern was that Dr. Gómez and his collaborators would exhibit the right spirit and attitude towards those who use the RV 1909 and 1960.

Dr. Zeinner has been very familiar with the controversy over the Spanish Bible for many years, having spent twenty-nine years (with only one furlough) as a church-planting missionary in Mexico.

As Dr. Zeinner, who is fluent in Spanish, investigated the RVG he was pleased with not only the text but also Dr. Gómez's spirit and attitude. Not only did Bearing Precious Seed print the first edition under the leadership of Dr. Zeinner, but since then Dr. Zeinner has become a very strong supporter of the revision.

Today, Dr. Zeinner operates a ministry that aids Bible translators around the world, called Bearing Precious Seed Global.

THE ROLE OF
JIM AND TIM FELLURE

Dr. Gómez approached Jim Fellure, who is the director of Victory Baptist Press, in Milton, Florida, a ministry of Victory Baptist Church. His son, Tim Fellure, is the pastor there.

The Fellures were immediately interested in printing the RVG. But before deciding, they were careful to investigate it, and rightfully so.

Both Fellures were so interested that they, along with another pastor from Florida, went all the way to Matamoros, Mexico to personally ask some questions. Jim Fellure also sent copies of the text to Dr. D. A. Waite and Dr. Rex Cobb for their input.

Dr. Waite examined the RVG with Scrivener's 1894 edition of the Greek New Testament. Upon his first investigation he found everything to be in conformity to the Textus Receptus with the exception of one verse of Scripture which Dr. Gómez immediately corrected.

Dr. Waite also requested about ten more copies of the RVG to distribute amongst several of his colleagues for further examination.

Dr. Rex Cobb also did extensive studies comparing not only the RVG but several other major editions of the Reina-Valera Spanish Bible. His studies revealed how many times each version departed from the Textus Receptus:

- The 1569 departed 75 times.
- The 1602 departed 57 times.
- The 1862 departed 118 times.

- The 1865 departed 28 times.
- The 1909 departed 122 times.
- The 1960 departed 191 times.
- The 2001 departed 69 times.
- **The RVG 2010 departed zero times.**

Dr. Cobb's studies have been a great help to many.

From then on, both Dr. Waite and Dr. Cobb became not only strong supporters but also collaborators in the RVG revision to further purify it. Their expertise and experience proved to be valuable assets.

Dr. Gómez testifies:

> We were honored to have their assistance and, most of all, their friendship.

Shane Rice, a missionary in Peru and another of Dr. Gómez's collaborators, worked hard to make this Bible available for computer Bible programs such as E-sword, Sword Searcher, Bible Works, Power Bible, and many others.

The first edition was not only released in printed form but also over the Internet. Having the RVG on the Internet proved to be very instrumental in raising both the interest and involvement of many brethren around the world who came to support this effort.

A WORLDWIDE COLLABORATION

In 2004, this statement was posted on the Internet on the official website of the Dean Burgon Society and several other websites:

> Here it is for you to read and examine. If you can find anything in it that does not line up

with the Textus Receptus, or if you can find anything that is not written in good and perfect Spanish, we will immediately correct it for the good of our people and for the glory of the Lord. If any of you come up with a revision that proves to be better than ours, more perfect, more accurate, we will move aside and rally around it because this issue is not about us or you. It is about God's Word for the benefit of our people and for the salvation of this lost and dying world.

This was Dr. Gómez's policy from the beginning. This open policy is what differentiated his work from other revision projects. Dr. Gómez valued the input, both negative and positive, of God's people, no matter who they were or where they came from.

The international nature of this work helped speed up the process of doing a thorough revision since 2004.

The Church of Jesus Christ was the proving grounds. This was not the work of a Bible Society. Hispanic brethren in Spanish-speaking Bible-believing churches all over the world, who have adopted this Bible as their own, constantly proved this work as they read, studied, meditated, preached, and taught from it.

For years, Dr. Gómez fielded the valuable input of the brethren either via email, on the phone, or in person. Every time someone contacted him with a concern, observation, criticism, or suggestion, he says, "We set our pride aside to seriously consider their input."

Dr. Gómez did not incorporate every change that was recommended. Many times he and his collaborators found recommendations for changes to be unnecessary. But Dr. Gómez says, "As God is our witness, we thoroughly considered everyone's concern."

> The LORD gave the word: great was the company of those that published it.[51]

It would be impossible to give an exact number of all who collaborated. Hundreds of people corresponded with Dr. Gómez since the year 2000 with suggestions of changes, confirmation of accuracy, observations, and questions as a result of their own examination of the RVG through their personal studies, analysis, and usage of the RVG.

In this chapter, a few of these helpful individuals will be mentioned.

All of those who collaborated with Dr. Gómez are fluent in Spanish. Most are bilingual, fluent in both Spanish and English.

Some collaborators only speak Spanish and therefore their assistance was limited to ensure the accuracy of grammar and spelling in Spanish. Others are fluent in several languages and helped by comparing the text alongside Bibles in other languages.

I am not advocating compromise over fundamental truths and I am certainly not talking about the abomination of ecumenism. However, I am happy to see so many Christians working together who have sought for unity amongst those

---

51) Psalm 68:11.

who share similar convictions in regards to the need for a totally pure Spanish Bible.[52]

It needs to be emphasized that though *every* man that assisted Dr. Gómez stands for the King James Bible in English and the Reina-Valera Gómez in Spanish, not all of them see eye to eye on every issue. At any rate, God gave Dr. Gómez and his collaborators the grace to set their differences aside long enough to realize that God's Word is much bigger than their egos.

Dr. Gómez was willing to listen to what all had to say concerning the text, for he felt that objectivity was essential in order to accomplish the goal of a completely accurate Spanish Bible.

The technicalities, semantics, and small issues that would otherwise hinder some from working together in unity did not prohibit Dr. Gómez and his collaborators from accomplishing something great for the glory of God and the good of His people.

This revision was not the work of a society, although men who are members of various Bible societies assisted. This revision was not the result of a committee of elitists, although some men who are definitely experts in different areas were involved.

This Bible is not even the fruit of only those in the ministry. Many laypersons participated. And throughout the process, the input of everyone from the pew to the pulpit was regarded as equally important.

---

52) Psalm 133:1, Ephesians 4:3.

God's Word does not belong to a society, or a committee of experts, or a pool of Fundamentalist leaders. It belongs to the church of Jesus Christ, which is the pillar and ground of the truth. It belongs to the royal priesthood of believers. It belongs to the least esteemed as well as the highly regarded and well respected.

The Bible is God's gift to every born-again Christian that ever knelt before Calvary's cross to find eternal redemption for their souls. And the ground is still level at the foot of the cross.

I would like to mention some of the men who assisted Dr. Gómez in this work. It is important to note that every one of these men is a Bible-believing Christian. Each one believes in the verbal, plenary inspiration and preservation of the scriptures.

They believe in the superiority of the Received Texts as opposed to the Alexandrian Critical Texts. And every one of these men stands for the KJV as the preserved Word of God in English without error.

As I was compiling this list of men, I could not help but notice something very interesting. Almost all of these men are *church planters*. And without exception, they are *all* passionate *soul winners!*

This is very significant. The men God sent to assist Dr. Gómez in this great task are *all* deeply involved in the work of God.

I do not believe this is a coincidence. This shows the type of people that God uses to accomplish anything for His name's sake.

God was not looking for big names. He brought qualified men, gifted in languages and linguistics. He used men who are born again, with a servant's heart, a passion for souls and a burning desire to take the glorious Gospel to a lost and dying world.

They are men of action. They are soldiers of the cross! These are the kind of men God uses to cause His Word to grow and multiply.

Most modern Bibles today are the product of men who are either trying to make a name for themselves or are trying to make a buck.

None of the men who participated in the RVG project was paid to do so. Most of them communicated their desire to not even be mentioned as Dr. Gómez's collaborators, not because they feared the criticism of those who disagree with this work but rather they did not wish for others to think of them more highly than they ought to think.

These men are humble servants of the Lord who simply wanted a pure Bible for use in their personal lives and to minister to others. And yes, they ARE using it to bring sinners to Jesus, to start and establish churches, and to stir up God's people to serve Him.

Here are some of these men:

CARLOS DONATE

Carlos Aníbal Donate Alvira graduated Magna Cum Laude from high school in Ft. Buchanan, Puerto Rico in 1980.

He graduated with honors (Summa Cum Laude and 4.0 GPA) from Hyles Anderson College in 1984 with a Bachelor of Science in Missions. That same year he was ordained into the Gospel ministry by the late Dr. Jack Hyles at the First Baptist Church in Hammond, Indiana.

He worked under Bill Rice Ranch Missions (to the deaf) from August of 1984 through May of 1989.

Since 1990 he has served as a missionary in Guatemala, South America. During his time in Guatemala, God used him to start the following ministries:

- Efata Baptist Mission for the Deaf, Guatemala (1991-1995)
- Efata Baptist Church, Guatemala City (1996-present)
- The Cross Baptist Mission, Santa Rosa, Guatemala (1998-present)
- Socorro Baptist Mission, Santa Lucia, Guatemala (1999-2007)
- Biblical Foundation Baptist Church, Mixco, Guatemala (2000-2004)
- Fundamental Bible Baptist Institute, Guatemala City (1999-present). Five graduates are currently in full time Christian work pastoring churches in Guatemala and the USA.

In addition to his work on the mission field, Brother Donate has served as a visiting professor to Landmark Baptist College in Haines City, Florida, and Miami Baptist College in Miami, Florida.

He is a member of the Confraternity of Evangelical Fundamentalist Churches in Guatemala, and is an Advisory Council member of the Dean Burgon Society.

He has written numerous Gospel tracts and Bible study materials, and is the author of two books.[53]

Brother Donate is also a pioneer of the Spanish Bible issue. For many years he called for the revision of the Valera Bible. With his proficiency in the Greek and Hebrew languages, his fluency in Spanish, and his many years of experience on the foreign field, he was a huge help in ensuring the purity and accuracy of the text.

DR. DONALD A. WAITE

Dr. D. A. Waite was our resident scholar concerning the Greek and Hebrew languages. *No one* involved with the Spanish Bible issue today has more scholarship credentials than Dr. Waite in regards to the original languages. He has studied the original languages since 1945, and has five earned degrees in this area.

He received a Bachelor of Arts in classical Greek and Latin from the University of Michigan in 1948.

He graduated with high honors in New Testament Greek Literature and Exegesis from Dallas Theological Seminary in 1952. He went on to earn a Master of Arts degree in Speech from the Southern Methodist University in 1953, a Doctorate of Theology, with honors, in Bible Exposition from Dallas Theological Seminary in 1955, and a Ph.D in Speech from Purdue University in 1961. (That's a total of sixteen years of college studies!)

In addition to his extensive knowledge of the original

---

53) *LENSEGUA- El lenguaje de Señas de Guatemala,* and *La Restauración de la Biblia de Valera, 400 Años de Historia.*

languages and Latin, Dr. Waite also has formal training in French and Spanish. In fact, early in his ministry he spent two years pastoring a Spanish-speaking church.

Dr. Waite is licensed in two different states (New Jersey and Pennsylvania) for the instruction of Greek and Language Arts. Most language professors in Bible colleges today, as fine as their abilities may be, do not have the official certifications by their state to teach the original languages. But Dr. Waite does.

He has taught Greek, Hebrew, Speech, English, and Bible courses in one junior high school, one senior high school, three Bible institutes, two colleges, two universities, and one seminary (nine schools altogether).

Today Dr. Waite serves as the pastor of the Bible For Today Baptist Church in Collingswood, New Jersey.

He is also a noted author of many books defending the KJV and Received Texts. His book, *Defending the King James Bible,* is a classic.

Perhaps he is best known as the president and founder of the Dean Burgon Society, a society of men committed to the study and defense of traditional Bible texts.

Dr. Waite and his society are not only strong supporters of the RVG, but they were a "right arm" in this work when it came to ensuring that the RVG Bible conformed to the Received Texts.

Although Dr. Waite was certainly not the only consultant on this project concerning Greek or Hebrew questions, every question or concern with the text that required knowledge of Greek or Hebrew grammar was brought to his attention.

So in regards to the original languages, he served as the primary consultant.

DR. REX COBB

Dr. Cobb began his training for the Gospel ministry at Midwestern Baptist College in Pontiac, Michigan, in 1970 (when the late Dr. Tom Malone was the President of the college), and graduated from FaithWay Baptist Institute in Ypsilanti, Michigan, in 1973.

That same year he and his wife, Mary, began attending the Baptist Bible Translators Institute in Bowie, Texas. They graduated from there in 1975, then moved to Bogotá, Colombia in 1976 where they studied Spanish at the Universidad Javeriana until 1978.

The Cobbs then served as missionaries in Mexico until 1999 (a total of 21 years). Rex was granted an honorary Doctor of Divinity degree for his accomplishments at Landmark Baptist College in Haines City, Florida, in 2008.

Dr. Cobb now serves as the director of Baptist Bible Translators Institute in Bowie, Texas, where he and his staff train missionaries from all over the world in advanced linguistic studies for the purpose of translating the scriptures into foreign languages.

Dr. Cobb is not just a teacher. He also has practical experience in what he teaches. While serving as a missionary in Mexico, he became burdened for the Zapotecas Indians in Oaxaca. These people had no Bible, so he took it upon himself to translate the entire New Testament into their language.

As a result, this faithful man has firsthand experience

in Bible translation and now trains other missionaries to do the same.

Dr. Cobb spent hundreds of hours collating sixteen different editions of the Spanish Bible, comparing them to the Textus Receptus. He concluded that the RVG is the purest and most accurate Spanish Bible available.

Dr. Gómez had the benefit of gleaning from Dr. Cobb's knowledge during this revision. Dr. Cobb testifies that he has fallen in love with the RVG so much that he now uses it for his personal daily morning devotions. It was a great blessing to have men like this going through the revision on a daily basis.

JOSEPH MARTINEZ

Brother Joe Martinez was born in Cuba. He graduated from Tabernacle Baptist College in Greensville, South Carolina (when the late Dr. Harold Sightler was the pastor and president there).

Brother Joe is a zealous soul winner. He has worked in a church-planting ministry to Hispanics throughout the southeastern part of the United States for the past sixteen years. During that time he has planted four churches:

- Chilhowie, VA - Iglesia Bautista Solo Cristo Salva
- Gray, TN - Iglesia Bautista Calvario
- Monroe, NC – Iglesia Bautista Victoria
- Newport, NC –Iglesia Bautista la Gracia

DAVID W. DANIELS

Brother David Daniels is the Research Consultant at Chick Publications. Everyone is familiar with the Gospel literature of Chick Publications, especially their famous Chick tracts, which have been used worldwide in over 100 languages to bring souls to Jesus Christ.

Brother Daniels graduated in 1984 from the Pacific Christian College (now Hope International University) in Fullerton, California, with a B.A. in Linguistics and Bible.

In 1986 he finished a three-summer course at the Summer Institute of Linguistics (associated with Wycliffe Bible Translators).

In 1987 he received his Master of Divinity in General Theology from Fuller Theological Seminary in Pasadena, California.

He is also a noted author. His books include *Babylon Religion*, *Did The Catholic Church Give Us The Bible?*, *Answers To Your Bible Version Questions*, and a pamphlet defining uncommon words in the KJV called *The King James Bible Companion*.

A few years ago a concerned missionary contacted Brother Daniels and asked if Chick Publications would consider using the RVG in their tracts in Spanish. Brother Daniels, who knows Spanish, researched the RVG for himself and distributed copies to several Spanish-speaking workers on staff with Chick Publications for investigation.

They brought several concerns regarding the text to Dr. Gómez's attention. But overall they were very pleased with what they saw. Dr. Gómez seriously analyzed every observation from Chick Publications and made the adjustments wherever needed.

Today all literature in Spanish by Chick Publications is

being revised, using the RVG as their official Spanish Bible, thanks to David Daniels and his research team.

REYNALDO VILLAREAL JR.

Brother Villareal graduated from Bob Jones University in 1983 with a BA degree. In addition, he has two years of graduate school.

From 1986 to 1993, he served in a local church as a deacon, associate pastor, in the nursing home ministry, and as the missions director.

Around 1992 he was called to Mexico to serve as a church-planting missionary. And since 1996 Brother Villareal and his family have served in Mexico.

MICHAEL LEMMA

Brother Lemma graduated from Hyles Anderson College in 1991 (Cum Laude) with a Bachelor of Science in Missions. He was ordained into the Gospel ministry by the late Dr. Jack Hyles at the First Baptist Church of Hammond, Indiana, on November 19, 1994.

After two-and-half years of deputation, he attended language school in Monterrey, Mexico at Mount Hebron Baptist Church from September 1998 to May 1999. Since then he has been used of God to plant the following churches:

- Independent Baptist Church of Zacatecas, Zacatecas (August 1999-2008). He handed over the work to one of his trained men.
- Independent Baptist Church of Jerez, Zacatecas (September 2003-August 2005). He handed over the work to one of his trained men.

111 GOD'S BIBLE IN SPANISH

- Independent Baptist Church of Fresnillo, Zacatecas, started by one of his trained men in April 2007.
- He is currently establishing a fourth church, in Ciudad Victoria, Tamaulipas.

Brother Lemma was a tireless worker in this revision. He went through every verse of the RVG from Genesis to Revelation and compared it with the KJV. He also compiled an exhaustive chart comparing the RVG, KJV, and the major revisions of the Spanish Bible. This chart appears in Appendix A.

NELSON GIMENEZ

Brother Gimenez has lived in Paraguay, South America all of his life. He was led to the Lord and trained for the ministry by missionary Mike Wilps, another avid supporter of the RVG.

Brother Gimenez is fluent in three languages, Spanish, English, and Guarani (a Paraguayan Indian dialect – Paraguay's second official language). His services as a professional translator of legal documents and as an interpreter is requested by several companies and international organizations in Paraguay.

He serves as the pastor of Bible Baptist Church in Villeta, Paraguay. Pastor Gimenez thoroughly examined the RVG text and uses it daily to minister to God's people and win Paraguayan souls to Jesus.

SHANE RICE

Brother Shane Rice was born and raised in a Christian home. His father, Ed Rice, is the pastor of Good Samaritan

Baptist Church in Dresden, New York. He was saved at the early age of five and surrendered to preach the Word of God at age 13. All his life he was very interested in missions.

Upon graduation from high school, he spent the entire summer in Peru. While there, God called him to be a missionary to that country.

Shane graduated from Massillon Baptist College (where the late Dr. Bruce Cummons was the president) with a Bachelor of Divinity in 1997. He married Kathy in January of 1998 and they headed to Peru in October of 2002.

They spent one year in language school and the next two years working with Efata Baptist Church in Lima, Peru. While in Efata they learned sign language.

After a furlough they returned to Cajamarca, Peru, where God used them to start Anchor Baptist Church in March of 2007.

Brother Rice is an Advisory Council member of the Dean Burgon Society, and was very instrumental in promoting the RVG and making it available through electronic means by formatting it for many computer programs.

He also created the official Reina-Valera Gómez website: www.reinavaleragomez.com.

ULISES VELAZQUEZ GALINDO

Brother Ulises was born and raised in Durango, Mexico. He started out in the ministry as a traveling street preacher. After street preaching in every state in Mexico, he eventually settled down in Alcodones. Since then he has started a church in Alcodones as well as a Spanish ministry in Yuma, Arizona.

Brother Ulises, a fervent soul winner, currently pastors both of those ministries. He also operates a website in Spanish that provides Bible studies, Sunday school material, and theological topics he has translated into Spanish: www.interbiblia.com.

Not only did Brother Ulises investigate the RVG and compare it to other Spanish Bibles, he also assisted in formatting the bilingual edition of the RVG (with the KJV parallel). He and several others worked on the template for the cross reference edition of the RVG.

DONALD HEINZ

Brother Heinz received his bachelor's degree from Maranatha Baptist Bible College in 1989. He received his Master's degree from Great Plains Baptist Divinity School in 1993 through his studies at Baptist Bible Translators Institute, where he was trained in advanced linguistic studies and Bible translating principles.

He has served as a church-planting missionary in Chile, South America for many years, and has a website in Spanish (www.palabraspuras.wordpress.com) where he and his colleague, Gary Castner, a veteran missionary in Chile, discuss in depth the textual changes and differences of the Spanish Bibles.

OTHERS WHO HELPED

Space does not allow us to provide a detailed background and the full credentials of everyone who had a part in the RVG project, but others who helped include:

• **Vincente Delgado**: A native Spaniard, layman in Spain.

- **Dr. Pedro Almeida:** A Brazilian pastor.
- **Jose Martinez:** (not to be confused with Joseph Martinez.) Jose is bilingual, and has been a veteran missionary in Argentina for over twenty years.
- **Elson Portugal:** A native Brazilian, he is fluent in English, Spanish, Portuguese, and German. He is also a veteran missionary and Church planter in Germany, Brazil, and Costa Rica.
- **Ole Olson:** Half Mexican, half Jew, he speaks English, Spanish, and Hebrew. He proofread the entire New Testament of the second edition in just two months.
- **Ruben de la Rosa:** A native of Mexico, he is an Engineer of Communications, a Sunday School superintendant, and a lay preacher.
- **Don Rich:** A bilingual, veteran missionary in Peru.
- **Juan Riquelme:** Hispanic, veteran missionary in Chile.
- **Antoni Mendoza Miralles:** Hispanic preacher in Spain.
- **Ricardo Monteagudo:** Hispanic preacher in Argentina.
- **Gary Castner:** A bilingual, veteran missionary in Chile, who has written many articles in Spanish on the different Spanish Bibles (www.palabraspuras.wordpress.com.)
- **Jose Luis Nuñez:** A native Mexican, and a pastor in Mexico for over thirty years.
- **Alex Holawaty:** A native Argentinean, and a veteran Pastor in Paraguay.

Most of the men listed here are ministers. We haven't even begun to mention the countless Christians in the congregations of these ministers who also proved the RVG text in their own personal studies.

Collectively, these people and many more around the world read and re-read the RVG text and communicated their thoughts to Dr. Gómez.

THE CONTRIBUTION OF
THE CRITICS

No work can be qualified as intellectually honest without the serious consideration of the opposing viewpoint. Dr. Gómez's most outspoken critics, who worked hard to discredit his efforts, have also proven to be valuable resources in ensuring accuracy.

As was stated on the official website on January 23, 2008:

Criticism has forced us to seek perfection. The stronger the criticism, the more it requires of us to do a better job. Criticism is very healthy. It points to our mistakes (which have been many). By the grace of God we have been man enough to admit our mistakes and correct them. Often, our critics have contributed more than the ones that applaud our work. I recommend for you to read what they have to say. You may learn something.[54]

Although the objections of the critics were very harsh, Dr. Gómez thanks God for all that they contributed.

Of course, it is important to note that most of the criticism came, not because of a desire to make the RVG the

---

54) Dr. Humberto Gómez, *My Opinion about Our Critics.*

best Bible it could be, but rather because the critics had a vested interest in another Bible revision.

Several times those who disapproved of Dr. Gómez's efforts had their minds made up from day one that they would never support his work. Because of that, they produced long lists of verses trying to point out deficiencies in the RVG text.

To whoever they could, they would mass mail articles that included these lists in hopes of discouraging others from supporting the RVG.

Many times the items they listed were not even textual issues but simply disagreements with the choices of wording Dr. Gómez came up with, despite the fact that his choices, though admittedly debatable at times, were not in conflict with the Received Texts or the KJV. Many times they simply tried to make "a mountain out of a molehill."

One brother who believed the Bible revision he supported was better than the RVG compiled a list of over 300 places where he disagreed with the RVG. Rather than simply discarding the list, Dr. Gómez emailed it to several of his main collaborators, who thoroughly went through each complaint one by one.

Most of these so-called errors were readings from the first edition that had already been changed. Most of them were non-issues to begin with.

Nevertheless, Dr. Gómez and his collaborators objectively considered every single complaint, and as a result of all their effort, they did find at least two items that warranted a second look.

Though most of the criticism was irrelevant, the opposition held Dr. Gómez's feet to the fire and for that he is very grateful.

WHY IS IT COPYRIGHTED?

Some well-meaning, sincere Christians have expressed concern about the fact that the RVG has a copyright. Many of these good brethren fail to realize that the KJV was also copyrighted during the days of its inception and for good reason. As one author points out:

> For the purposes of protecting the text, the King James Version of the Bible was originally copyrighted and still is in the United Kingdom. The rights to print this Bible were granted to several publishing houses over the centuries. Today, however, for the rest of the world the King James Bible text is free of copyright restrictions.
>
> This entire approach is quite different from the copyrights held today on modern Bible versions. The modern versions are tightly controlled by secular publishing empires for the primary purpose of revenue.[55]

Just as the KJV, the RVG was copyrighted to protect the text so that no one can make changes in it. Dr. Gómez explains:

> We want our Bible to be available to all but

---

55) Dr. R. B. Ouellette, *The More Sure Word*, p. 149.

we do not want it to be open for anyone to
start making changes of their own to the text.[56]

Dr. Gómez has indicated that all financial gains from his
sale of leather-bound RVG Bibles will be used to print more
Bibles. In fact, any Bible printing ministry has the liberty to
print the RVG without even asking for permission, so long
as they do not change the text.

Hence, the copyright.

---

56) Email correspondence.

CHAPTER 6

Removing Hell from the Bible

By Missionary Shane Rice

Hell is a hot topic in and of itself but when the issue of the Spanish Bible is thrown on top, discussion tends to become ever more heated.

One may believe in hell his entire life. However it is not his belief in hell that makes it real. What the Bible teaches about hell is what makes it real. It is important to note the difference.

What one believes strongly sways his interpretation of passages. Somewhere along the line, it must be determined that the Bible is not to be interpreted based on one's values or belief system, but rather what is actually written plainly and clearly in the Word of God.

Hell is a *fundamental doctrine* upon which the rest of

the doctrines hinge. It traces back through the Waldenses all the way to the Apostles and to the very doctrine of Jesus Christ. It should not be taken lightly.

If there is no hell, there is no need for salvation. After all, people are saved from eternal punishment, not the grave where life ceases to exist. There is a device that diminishes the doctrine of hell from the Word of God. One must keep his eyes open and be aware of such attacks.

THE DANGERS OF TRANSLITERATION

We will now discuss how transliteration affects the Word of God. The poor usage of transliteration will be considered, as well as some needed places for transliteration.

The way *sheol* was translated in the Old Testament will be examined as well as the three Greek New Testament words that are dealt with by this topic.

Lastly, we will look at the pattern set by the modern Bibles and the modern Bible societies.

Why does the King James Bible uses the word "hell" 54 times, while most modern versions use it less than 15 times? Has this problem seeped into foreign language Bibles? How do the common Spanish Bibles stand up in this battle? On which side of the fence do they fall? All of these questions will be dealt with in this chapter.

Transliteration is simply defined as:

> ...to change letters, words, etc. into corresponding characters of another alphabet or language.

That means the Greek word, ᾽αδης would be transliterated to *Hades* in the English language. Many words and names have been adopted into the English language that were originally just transliterated words. Thus Μαρκος transliterates into *Markos* and is the root of the name "Mark."

The problem with transliteration is that it tends to lose the meaning. "Mark" probably originates from the Latin, *Markus*. It is easy to see its form in the Greek and how it closely relates to the English name "Mark." It has a few meanings depending on what language is used as the base, or root language.

So transliteration is taking the word from the original language and writing its equivalent letters in the receptor language. The meaning then takes the meaning from the original language. This is best and most often done when no word in the receptor language carries the same definition.

However, when a word is transliterated into a language that already has a word that matches the definition of the original word, some questions must be asked. What is the advantage/disadvantage of transliterating this word? Will the people of the receptor language understand the transliterated word? What is the motive behind transliterating?

OLD TESTAMENT TRANSLITERATION

Strong's Concordance defines the Hebrew word *sheol* as:

> From H7592; *hades* or the world of the dead (as if a subterranean {*retreat*}) including its accessories and *inmates*: - {grave} {hell} pit.

The last part of Strong's definition shows the three ways the word was translated in the KJV, "grave," "hell," and "pit." The word *sheol* is found 65 times in the Old Testament. Of those, it is translated 31 times as "grave," 31 times as "hell," and only 3 times as "pit."

First of all, the word "hell" (*infierno*) cannot be found in the Old Testament of the Reina-Valera 1960 Spanish Bible. This is not an accident or a coincidence.

In the RV 1909 one can find the word *infierno* 13 times in the Old Testament, whereas in the RV 1865 *infierno* can be found 20 times. However in the Old Testament of the King James Bible and the Reina-Valera Gómez Spanish Bible "hell" can be found 31 times.

Deuteronomy 32:22 is the first time that *sheol* was translated as "hell" in the King James Bible. It shouldn't come as a surprise that both the William Tyndale Bible and the John Wycliffe Bible both agree with the KJV.

In the Spanish Bible it is *profundo*, which means "the deep" or "pit." This isn't such a problem, since at the time, Reina and Valera were running for their very lives from the Roman Catholic church, who wanted to destroy their translation work.

So when minor problems like this are encountered in their translation, it is understandable since they were under such dire circumstances. They should still be held in high esteem and respected for the admirable work they did. If they had been afforded the opportunity to see how others had translated this verse, perhaps they would have re-thought the final words.

It is also very interesting to note that the Strong's Hebrew word H8482 means "lowest" or *profundo* and then the next Strong's word is the Hebrew word *sheol*, therefore just translating it as *profundo* would leave a word untranslated, thus omitting a word from the text.

Notice how it is written in the King James Bible: "unto the lowest (H8482) hell (H7585 – *sheol*)."

In 2 Samuel 22:6 we also see an interesting development in Spanish Bible history. The 1602 reads *hueffa*, using the old style lettering much like the original 1611 King James Bible. The letter "f" is sometimes used for an "s," making this read *huessa* or *huesa* today, carrying the same meaning as "sepulcher", which is how the 1865 reads. Instead of the "sorrows of hell" it reads "the sorrows of the sepulcher" or grave "compassed me about."

However, the 1909 revisers changed the word to *infierno* (hell.) They must have come to a legitimate conclusion that this word should be translated as "hell."

Then the RV 1960 revision committee removed this word, taking a step backwards by putting the transliterated word *sheol* in place of "hell." With *sheol* (or *seol* in Spanish) replacing the word "hell," it is now up to the reader to figure out what this word means. Should it be "grave," "pit" or "hell?"

When qualified scholars, with the time and protection that the King James translators had, decided it should be "hell," who in this day and age is qualified to argue with them?

The revisers of the RV 1960 decided it should be left up to the average lay people, Sunday school teachers, and preachers to figure it out for themselves.

Going to a Spanish dictionary isn't much help as the word *seol* is not a Spanish word and doesn't show up in the most prominent Spanish dictionary (*The Real Academia Española*).

Transliterating this word does nothing to shed light on the interpretation or understanding of this passage. This is not a step forward for a revision, but a step backwards. Why not just have the people learn Hebrew and forget about translating it altogether. Job 11:8 reads:

> It is as high as heaven; what canst thou do?
> deeper than hell; what canst thou know?

This is a particularly interesting verse in the history of the Spanish Bible. Those who hold so strongly to the RV 1960 would lead others to believe that it says the same as the 1602 original. But this is not so. For well over 400 years, *sheol* was translated *infierno* or "hell" until the 1900s when the committee of the RV 1960 decided to replace *infierno* with the transliteration of the word.

What could be the purpose of such a decision? The translators and revision committees for the past 400 years all agreed that this word should be translated "hell."

The same question could be asked about Job 26:6, Psalm 55:15, Proverbs 15:11, Isaiah 14:9, Ezekiel 32:21 and Amos 9:2.

Another interesting verse is Psalm 139:8:

> If I ascend up into heaven, thou art there: if I
> make my bed in hell, behold, thou art there.

In 1602 they correctly translated this word *infierno* or "hell." In 1865 it stayed as well. However, in 1909 they decided to change it to *abismo* which primarily means "pit," though it could possibly mean "hell." Why, after 400 years of the accurate *infierno*, did they decide to change it to "pit?"

Then there is the RV 1960 sticking to its "new age" pattern of replacing this word with the Hebrew transliteration. Shame on the 1909 and the 1960 for replacing this perfectly fine translation after 400 years of being correct with an inaccurate word.

"If I make my bed in a pit?" What pit? It is very unspecific and unclear. "If I make my bed in hell," is a specific place that everyone knows about, a much clearer reading.

In Proverbs 15:24 there is yet another interesting fact. The 1602 and 1865 went with *sima* or "pit." However the RV 1909 decided to fix this, and correctly translate it *infierno*.

One might ask, "What determines if the word should be translated as "hell?" Or "What makes the English translation in this passage superior to that of another translation?" These are both valid questions. Some of the most heated discussions come over this very point.

Let it be stated in a simple manner. The KJV translators had all the comfort of sitting under the protection of a King and kingdom. They had the luxury of having over fifty absolute scholars work together on the project. They had the time necessary to do the work.

They were able to get all the manuscripts and materials they needed. They could consult other preserved translations and see how they were translated. It is highly likely that they even consulted the Reina-Valera 1602 Spanish Bible.

This does not by any means slight Reina and Valera or their work. Reina and Valera worked at separate times, not side by side. They both were running for their very lives while working on the translation.

Both were very well versed in the Biblical languages, and perhaps would have been a welcomed pair to the team of translators who worked on the KJV. However, they didn't have all the luxuries the KJV translators enjoyed.

So verses in the Reina-Valera needed to be fixed, not because the translators were unfaithful, but because they were under desperate circumstances and had limited time to work on the manuscripts.

Their work is to be applauded and held in high esteem because they worked faithfully with what they had.

Given the two overviews of the histories, it should be best to take the King James translators over Reina and Valera's original work.

Just a few other Old Testament examples will be sufficient to make the point that there is a problem with the most common Spanish Bibles. Ezekiel 31:16 in the KJV says:

> I made the nations to shake at the sound of his
> fall, when I cast him down to hell with them
> that descend into the pit: and all the trees of
> Eden, the choice and best of Lebanon, all that
> drink water, shall be comforted in the nether
> parts of the earth.

This is similar to Psalm 139:8, where the RV 1909 starts the downhill slide. This verse is correct in the 1602 and the 1865. However the 1909 changes *infierno* (hell) to "grave." Once again, for 400 years it was fine, then they decided to change it.

We also see that the RV 1960 sticks true to its pattern of changing every instance to *seol,* the transliteration of the Hebrew word. The same thing can be said about Jonah 2:2 in the 1909 and the 1960 Spanish Bibles.

This well known verse has been discussed throughout the ages. Obviously, bodies in the grave cannot pray or call out to God. Hence the accurate translation says, "out of the belly of hell cried I." Whether he was physically in hell or not, his body was not in a grave if he was alive. So "hell" is the accurate translation.

If one does not agree with this argument, the 50-plus men who translated the KJV could certainly present a better argument for their reasoning. But it can be noted that in Luke 16 a man is crying out from hell, not from the grave.

One more example to look at: Habakkuk 2:5:

> Yea also, because he transgresseth by wine, he
> is a proud man, neither keepeth at home, who
> enlargeth his desire as hell, and is as death, and
> cannot be satisfied, but gathereth unto him
> all nations, and heapeth unto him all people:

In this verse the 1602, as well as the 1865, put *osario,* which means "a bone pit" (where they put the bones of people that were buried.)

The RV 1909 changed this to *infierno,* which is our English word "hell." Imagine that! Those who stand firmly on the KJV had nothing to do with that decision.

It is just observed one hundred years after the fact, and can be recognized that a conscious decision was made to put the word "hell" back into the text.

On the other hand, the RV 1960 once again removed that word and put their transliteration into the verse.

Looking back over the Old Testament, it should not be a surprise that the RV 1960 is not the only Bible that transliterates the word "hell." The American Standard Version in English does the same thing. It was put together in 1901, about fifty years before the RV 1960 was even started.

It isn't a coincidence that they are both put out by the American Bible Society. They are out to sell those Bibles. A certain amount of politics enter into their work so they can continue to make money, even if it means sacrificing truth on the altar of money. Just who are they serving?

Can there be named just one Bible that the American Bible Society has produced that is accurate and faithful to the Textus Receptus or Traditional texts? The answer is NO. They don't put out Bibles that are faithful and accurate to the Textus Receptus.

If they did, they would not be able to copyright them because they would have a Bible too similar to the KJV. This is not their desire or aim. So why should anyone believe that any Bible produced by them is correct?

In concluding the Old Testament, not one single time in the Old Testament can the word "hell" be found in the 1960 Reina-Valera Bible. They replaced it every time with the transliterated Hebrew word *sheol* (*seol* in Spanish.)

Remember that *seol* does not appear in the *Real Academia Española*[57] (equal to *Webster's Dictionary* in English as the

---

standard for dictionaries) or in any of its previous editions since the 1700s. One may happen across *seol* in other Spanish dictionaries, but this would not be normal. So the reader is left in the air every time he or she reads this word *seol*.

The 1909 and the 1865 do a decent job in their translation but are still lacking. It should come as a surprise that the New World Translation of the Jehovah's Witness does the same thing in their English and Spanish Bibles by transliterating every instance of the Hebrew word *sheol.*

The American Standard Version follows the same pattern. This seems to be a newer "modern" method, true in many "modern" Bibles, leaving the readers to determine what *sheol* means in their own tongue.

If the scholars on the translating team are unable to determine the proper context and meaning of the Hebrew word, then how is the common lay person supposed to come to an accurate conclusion?

NEW TESTAMENT TRANSLATION

The New Testament gets a little more attention concerning the doctrine of hell because several different words are translated "hell."

The most known word that is translated is the Greek word *Hades. Hades* is used eleven times in the KJV New Testament. Ten of those times it is translated "hell." In one instance (1 Corinthians 15:55) it is translated "grave."

Another Greek word that is translated as "hell" is *Gehenna,* which is used twelve times in the New Testament. Every occurrence is translated "hell" in the KJV.

The last and least disputed word is *tartaros*, which is found in 2 Peter 2:4. This word is translated in almost every Bible as "hell," except the New World Translation, which they transliterate "Tar´ta·rus," thus completely erasing any existence of "hell" from their Bible.

The first occurrences of "hell" in the KJV New Testament are in Matthew 5:22, 29, 30 and 10:28, which are also translated "hell" (*infierno*) in the 1865, 1909, and 1960 Spanish Bibles.

The 1602 Spanish Bible renders it as *quemadero* or "a place of burning," which is not far from the context, since hell is a place of burning. This translation would not present a problem for many people.

Though the Greek word *Gehenna* was used in these passages, the 1865, 1909, and 1960 revisers accepted that this word was translated as clearly and accurately as "hell." Even the American Bible Society did not have a problem with this translation as they too translated it "hell" in the American Standard Version.

In Mark 9:43, 45, 47 and Luke 12:5 there is an odd twist in the history of the Spanish Bible. The 1602 translates all these passages as they did in the previous verses discussed, *quemadero*.

However the 1865 replaced that with *infierno* or "hell," but the RV 1909 decided to transliterate this word *Gehenna!* This is a very questionable change, for even the 1960 revisers working with the American Bible Society disagreed with them and replaced the word with the correct term, *infierno*.

HADES: HELL OR GRAVE?

Moving on to another example, the first use of *Hades* in the KJV is in Matthew 11:23. *Hades* is only translated one of two ways, "hell" or "grave." It is translated "hell" the majority of times, and "grave" once.

This verse is particularly interesting, for the 1602, 1865, and 1909 all translate this word as *infierno*, which is "hell." However, the 1960 revisers transliterated this word as *Hades*.

First of all, it stood the test of time of over 400 years as a clear and understandable word in Spanish. Therefore, one must question why it was necessary to change it to a transliterated word that does not appear in the current edition or any previous edition of the *Real Academia Española* dictionary.

It does not help clarify the text, not one iota. It only serves to obscure the meaning of this word, and further bury the actual meaning of this verse. It is not for the better, but for the worse to transliterate this word, especially after it has stood such a test of time.

The same can be said of Matthew 16:18; Luke 10:15, 16:23; Acts 2:27, 2:31; Revelation 1:18, 6:8, 20:13, 14. Of all these verses, three stand out as prominent verses.

One is Luke 16:23, the account of the rich man and Lazarus. Verses 23-24 state:

> And in hell he lift up his eyes, being in torments, and seeth Abraham afar off, and Lazarus in his bosom. And he cried and said, Father Abraham, have mercy on me, and send Lazarus, that he may dip the tip of his finger in water,

and cool my tongue; for I am tormented in
this flame.

There is no clearer and more definite verse that talks of
hell than this one. The rich man lifted up his eyes being in
hell. He was not in a grave, or any other place than hell.

That is why he proclaimed, "I am tormented in this
flame." It is absolutely ludicrous to transliterate this as *Hades*.
It doesn't help anyone understand the verse; it only diminishes
the doctrine. It is very clear that this refers to hell. Even the
liberal group that produced the New International Version
decided this should be translated as "hell."

Another bothersome instance of their transliteration is
Revelation 20:13-14, which states:

And the sea gave up the dead which were in
it; and death and hell delivered up the dead
which were in them: and they were judged
every man according to their works. And death
and hell were cast into the lake of fire. This is
the second death.

For this familiar passage be transliterated to *Hades* after
it has stood for over 400 years in the Spanish Bible as "hell"
is an offensive effort to obscure the doctrine of hell in the
Bible. There can be no other good explanation for such an
act. It doesn't clarify the text or shed any light on it to use
the word *Hades* instead of "hell."

The last instance that really stands out is Matthew 16:18:
"the gates of *hell* shall not prevail against it." Of course, the
text is referring to the church.

A text that reads, "the gates of *Hades* shall not prevail

against it" is very vague. *Hades* is not a word in either English, or Spanish. One having been in church his whole life may be familiar with the word *Hades* but it still does not carry the effect or power as the word "hell."

How much less helpful it is for someone not familiar with Biblical Greek to read *Hades*. It is not the gates of the "grave" that won't prevail against the church, it is the gates of "hell" that shall not prevail against the church.

There can be no valid reason for yanking "hell" out of these verses and replacing it with *Hades*. It does not help.

Every place the word *Hades* is used in the New Testament, the RV 1960 transliterates the word, except for 1 Corinthians 15:55, where it is translated as "grave."

It is hard to explain why the translation committee of the RV 1960 transliterated *Hades* everywhere it had been translated as "hell" in the Spanish Bibles, and not transliterate where it is translated as "death." If they did not intend to obscure the doctrine of hell, then it would be interesting to know the motivation behind such erroneous changes.

The only other reason that could be assumed is to "sell" their Bible and make money. After all, who wants to read about hell since it is not a very pleasant doctrine to consider. However, it is *clearly* written in the Word of God, and should be preached and taught, because it is a truth.

2 PETER 2:4 EXPLAINED

One more passage will shed light on this topic and nail down the point of this study. The Greek word *tartaros* only appears one time in the Scriptures, in 2 Peter 2:4:

> For if God spared not the angels that sinned,
> but cast them down to *hell*, and delivered them
> into chains of darkness, to be reserved unto
> judgment;

Strong's Concordance defines this word as:

> "From Ταρταρος, Tartaros (the deepest abyss
> of Hades); to incarcerate in eternal torment:
> —cast down to hell."

Notice that definition: "the deepest abyss of Hades." So if *tartaros* is the deepest abyss of Hades, and it is translated as "hell," would not it make sense to translate *Hades* as "hell?"

All of the Spanish Bibles from 1602 through 1960 translated this as "hell." Why not be consistent and translate *Hades* as "hell" as they did for over 400 years? Why change what the original Spanish translators placed in their text?

One article stated that the translation of these words was difficult and an area where translators were inconsistent. The article contended that it was more consistent to simply transliterate the Hebrew and Greek words instead of translating them. How intelligent is this?

So educated translators should refuse to translate the words so people can understand them? That would force every common lay person to learn Hebrew and Greek in order to learn the proper meaning.

They are saying that the 1960 revisers did the more noble thing. One has a right to that opinion. But if so, he should go to his home church and preach an entire message on hell, using only *Hades* or *sheol* and not mentioning "hell" even once. How much impact would that have?

Every preacher and missionary will stand before God and give account for the direction that he has led his people. We should not ask, "What did my preacher use?" or "What Bible was I given?" We need to ask, "What Bible communicates what God said in my language?"

Now is the time to stop and examine objectively the Bible translation that is being used and ask the Lord if it is the right Bible. Is it an accurate translation? Is it faithful to the Textus Receptus and Masoretic text, like the KJV?

MODERN BIBLES FOLLOW MODERN PATTERNS

Many modern Bibles follow a pattern. The KJV uses "hell" 54 times in the entire Bible. The Revised Standard Version only uses the word "hell" 13 times in the New Testament and zero times in the Old Testament, transliterating every instance with sheol.

The American Standard Version has done the same. In fact, the American Standard Version, the Revised Standard Bible, the Reina-Valera 1960, the Amplified Bible and the New American Standard Bible each use "hell" only 13 times. The English Standard Bible and the New International Version both only use "hell" 14 times.

The NIV recognized the foolishness of transliterating *Hades* in Luke 16:23, and the English Standard Version recognized the need to put "hell" into Matthew 16:18.

However the pattern is very real. Only thirteen instances of "hell" in the modern Bibles, whereas it can be found 54 times in the KJV.

Transliterating the word for "hell" obscures the doctrine of hell in modern Bibles. It has been a trend since the American Standard Version of 1901 that has caught on and started working its way into other languages. Prior to that, these words were translated, not transliterated.

Prior to the RV 1960, it was not common to transliterate in the Spanish language either. The Spanish Reina-Valera Actualizada of 1989, the RV 1995, and La Biblia de las Americas also only use the Spanish word for "hell" 13 times. The NIV in Spanish uses "hell" 17 times. Perhaps they recognized the need to put it back into the text.

This all demonstrates that there is a movement that is going in the wrong direction. There is no other clearly visible reason to move in this direction other than to make money, and greatly lessen the clear teaching of hell in the Bible.

CONCLUSION

It should not come as a surprise that the New World Translation that the Jehovah's Witnesses carry around with them transliterates every instance of the word *sheol, Hades, Gehenna,* and even *Tartaros.* Why?

The answer is simple, Jehovah's Witnesses don't believe in hell. They believe that when one dies, he goes to the grave. That is it, the end. The Spanish Bible has not gone to this extreme, however in what direction is it leaning?

The question asked previously need to be reiterated. "Why transliterate the words *sheol* and *Hades?*" Maybe these publishers and translators don't believe in hell, either.

A Bible that waters down the doctrine of hell leaves it up

to each individual reader to interpret the meaning of these Greek and Hebrew words. This is not what true Christians want.

For if it is left up to our own interpretation, then the Jehovah's Witnesses have every one of those verses to stand on, and we Bible-believers are left hanging in the air with a handful of verses that actually state "hell."

Whether the Bible is written in English, Spanish, French, Italian or any other language, all Christians must be wise to the fact that the world does not want to hear about, or believe in hell.

Many religions do not preach or teach on the doctrine of hell. They tiptoe around it and teach on other things, for if hell exists, then there are eternal consequences for their decisions here in this life. And if there are eternal consequences, then there is a *great need* for a Saviour!

Yes, there is a need. We must preach the pure Word.

The Spanish Bible down through the ages has continually decreased the use of the word "hell." In the 1602 Spanish Bible the word "hell" appears 31 times, while in the 1865 the word "hell" actually appears 43 times. The RV 1909 uses "hell" even less, just 30 times. Even worse, the RV 1960 uses the word "hell" a mere 13 times.

There is a major problem with this. The RV 1960 is not the same as the 1602 original work. Someone tampered with the text.

The Reina-Valera Gómez Bible is pure and accurate to the Textus Receptus and the Masoretic texts. If you are interested in a Spanish Bible that is pure, you would be more than happy to pick up a copy of the Reina-Valera Gómez Spanish Bible, and study it for yourself.

The RVG 2010 does not bend to the modern day pattern of transliterating the words *Hades* and *sheol*. It is very clear that hell is real. It follows the Traditional Texts like the King James does.

CHAPTER 7

Twenty Reasons a Veteran Hispanic Missionary Endorses the RVG

By Carlos Donate.

I endorse, support and use the Reina-Valera Gómez because of the following twenty facts:

1.

The RVG is based on the Antigua Reina-Valera 1909, which is the time-honored version of many fundamental, Bible-believing Hispanics. It was this, and not the RV 1960, which laid the foundation for fundamentalism in the Spanish world.

In honor of its legacy, the RVG faithfully honors the Bible-believing conservative and fundamental Spanish Christian world by maintaining much of its flavor and style.

2.

The Reina-Valera Gómez is the product of a serious biblical collation performed by Dr. Humberto Gómez, a Mexican national, and many other fundamental Baptist pastors and missionaries.

Dr. Gómez is a man of God that has dedicated the best years of his life to winning souls and planting churches in Mexico, his homeland. He has also been a blessing to many other Hispanic churches throughout Latin America and the USA, preaching revivals, missions conferences, and camp meetings.

His leadership role has been used of God to be a blessing to untold hundreds of Spanish-speaking pastors and missionaries. He has a definite dominion of his own native language, and he also has a working knowledge of the biblical languages.

However, what qualifies him to undertake this ministry more than anything else is his fear of God, and his absolute love for His holy words.

3.

The RVG is a faithful and accurate revision which follows the preserved manuscripts used by the KJV. Every verse of the Bible was carefully compared to the Masoretic Text in the Old Testament and the Received Text in the New Testament, removing every trace of corruption by modern textual criticism.

4.

The RVG is an answer to prayer to those of us who reject the ecumenical United Bible Societies' philosophies of translation. Years ago, I came to realize how the publications of the UBS have influenced modern textual scholarship, even in the Spanish world.

Dr. José Flores, a member of the Reina-Valera revision committee of 1960, said the 1960 introduced over 10,000 textual changes following the 1946 Revised Standard, the 1901 American Revised Standard, the English Revised Version of 1885, and the International Critical Commentary's liberal exegesis of the Scriptures.

According to Dr. Flores, their working principle was to do away with the Textus Receptus as much as possible and introduce more "contemporary" renderings of verses, as was recommended by the Translations Secretary, Mr. Eugene Nida.[58]

Originally, their intention was to update the language and introduce some good changes, but what they ended up with was a Valera Bible that was even farther departed from the Traditional Received Text.

5.

The RVG allows me to teach and preach with more authority on such vital issues as eternal retribution by properly translating the word *Hades, Gehenna* and *sheol*. Modern scholarship simply transliterates these words.

---

58) Dr. José Flores, *El Texto del Nuevo Testamento*, by CLIE, 1977, p. 232.

6.

The RVG allows me to teach and preach with a clearer and more authoritative text on the issue of inspiration and preservation as taught in Psalms 12: 6 and 7. The RVG translates the verses in such a way that the object of preservation was God´s holy words, and not the Jewish nation.

7.

The RVG renders Isaiah 9:3 without contradicting the KJV. The same reason applies to Isaiah 64:5, an important verse in the Old Testament that teaches security of the believer. Beginning in 1960, these and many other verses in the Old Testament were revised following modern textual scholarship.

8.

The RVG renders 1 Peter 3:21 properly, in agreement with the Traditional Received Text underlying the KJV, as "the like figure," speaking of baptism, whereas modern textual scholars omit this important phrase.

9.

The RVG, in agreement to the KJV, renders Revelation 19:8 as "the righteousness of saints" *(la justicia de los santos)* whereas modern textual scholarship, and the RV 1960 alludes to the works concept by rendering that phrase as "the just works of the saints" *(las acciones justas de los santos)*.

Compare the RV, ASV, RSV and the Latin Vulgate. They will agree with the RV 1960. The difference is that the RVG presents the word *justificaciones* as a noun, just like KJV's "righteousness," but the 1960 presents it as a verb, *acciones justas*. Big difference!

10.

In Exodus 12:5 the RVG properly translates the Hebrew word *seh* as lamb, leaving no doubt in the reader's mind that it is a reference to Christ, our sacrificial Lamb, while the RV 1960 calls it "the animal" in the first part of that verse. This is typical of Eugene Nida's method of dynamic equivalence.

11.

The RVG follows the Traditional Received Text by properly translating Luke 2:22. The verse is calling Mary unto purification, whereas modern textual scholarship, including the 1960 calls *both* Joseph and Mary unto purification.

12.

The RVG agrees with the KJV in 1 Thessalonians 4:4 by correctly translating the Greek word *skeous* as "vessel," which is one's body, not one's wife, otherwise the Holy Spirit would have said *guneh*.

13.

The RVG renders the Roman's Road to salvation right in Romans 10:9 just like the KJV as "that if thou shalt confess with thy mouth the Lord Jesus" whereas the 1960 renders it as the Westcott and Hort "Lordship-salvation" crowd does: "if thou shalt confess with thy mouth that Jesus *is Lord*."

14.

The RVG doesn't add the word "aspiration" in 1 Peter 3:21 like the RV 1960 does. Aspiring to be baptized is a pagan concept. See "New Age Bible Versions" by Dr. Gail Riplinger.

15.

The RVG follows the Traditional Received Text and the KJV closest in Revelation 22:14 by stating that "blessed is the man that doeth his commandments," whereas the RV 1960 has it just like the Westcott and Hort bibles, "blessed are they that wash their robes."

16.

The RVG follows the KJV properly in Luke 21:5 by using the word "gift," but the RV 1960 adds the Roman Catholic expression "votive" to "gifts." *Votive gifts* and *votive prayers* is popery!

17.

The RVG properly renders Psalm 2:12 as "*Kiss the Son*," whereas the 1960 changes it to "honor the son." This change weakens a vital cross-reference in Luke 7:45 where our Lord says about Simon's half-hearted devotion, "Thou gavest me no kiss." The kiss was the ultimate expression of love. There is union in a kiss. There is affection.

Though "honor" would seem to be a proper equivalent, the truth is that the Holy Spirit said *nashak*, which is literally "to kiss."

Dynamic equivalencies often alter the original meaning of a Hebrew or Greek word by taking into consideration the cultural significance.

Perhaps Mr. Nida and the revision committee thought that kissing the Son was something illogical, or impossible to do. But the fact remains that God said it, so that is how it must be translated.

We need to receive and believe every word the Author of Scripture said, and not change it because of our personal feelings.

18.

The RVG is correct like the KJV in Matthew 5:22 by rendering the phrase "without a cause" as *sin razón,* whereas the 1960 omits it altogether, following the Alexandrian Westcott and Hort.

Was our Lord Jesus guilty of sin when becoming angry in the Temple as He overthrew the thieves tables? According to the 1960, the ASV, RSV, RV, New World, etc, He was.

19.

The RVG has the endorsement of America's premier fundamentalist scholar, Dr. D.A. Waite, and the Dean Burgon Society. For decades, Dr. Waite has championed the cause of the defense of the Bible in English, the KJV, and those faithfully translated and revised with the proper texts and methodology.

20.

The RVG is being printed by Victory Baptist Press in Florida, as well as Chick Publications in California, plus at least seven other organizations from Brasil to South Korea to the United States. And the number keeps growing.

It is also being distributed by reputable ministries such as BEAMS (Baptist Evangelistic and Missionary Service), the Dean Burgon Society, the KJV Stores, and a growing list of

146 GOD'S BIBLE IN SPANISH

Christian organizations that want to get God's uncorrupted words into the hands of Spanish-speaking Christians.

These and many others are thanking God that we finally have a Bible in Spanish that lines up with the Traditional Received Text and the KJV in key passages.

Previous revisions of the Reina-Valera Bible attempted to do this, including the 1831, the 1865, and the 1909, but never revised it completely.

At last! The RVG finally fulfills the long awaited dream of providing an accurate revision of the Reina-Valera by the fundamentalist world.

CHAPTER 8

8 Reasons the President of a Bible Society Endorses the RVG

By Dr. Phil Stringer.

Dr. Stringer is the former Executive Vice-President of Landmark Baptist College in Haines City, Florida. He currently pastors Ravenswood Baptist Church in Chicago, Illinois. He is a noted speaker around the world, an author, and an Advisory Council member of the Dean Burgon Society. He is also the President of the William Carey Bible Society, a ministry that focuses on identifying and promoting foreign Bible translations based upon the Received Texts and the KJV as well as proper translating principles.

I have received a number of questions about why I support the Reina-Valera Gómez Bible —the new Spanish translation coordinated by Humberto Gómez.

I have also received several written criticisms of his work and have been asked to respond to them. The following is a summary of some key points on the subject.

1. I support the RVG because of its base text.

I believe that God inspired (breathed out) every word of the Scripture (Holy Writings). He used the Greek language, the Hebrew language and a little Aramaic to do so. These words became the standard for every translation in every language.

This is, by far, the most important standard for any translation effort. The purpose of any translation is to reproduce those original words in the language of the translation.

Dr. Gómez and those who worked with him were committed to the reproduction of those original words. Their base text was clearly designated. Throughout the various drafts of the work they remained open to have their work challenged on this basis.

Dr. Gómez believes that the accurate base text is the Received Text (Hebrew Masoretic text and the Greek Textus Receptus). This is the textual type used by faithful believers throughout the centuries.

I have not seen a single one of Dr. Gómez's critics state what they believe the base text for a Bible translation should be. If they do have a standard text, they are not making it known.

2. I support the RVG because it is based on sound doctrine.

Dr. Gómez and his collaborators believe in both the verbal, plenary inspiration of the Bible and the verbal preservation of the Scriptures. Their doctrinal position is clear and public.

Some of Dr. Gómez's best known independent Baptist critics believe in concept inspiration. I have heard some of them say this in person. I am not aware of what the rest believe, but they do not make their positions clear in their statements about the RVG.

3. I support the RVG because of those who created and endorse it.

Dr. D. A. Waite (the Dean Burgon Society) participated in the effort and endorsed the effort. His credentials speak for themselves:

(Note: *Here Dr. Stringer displays Dr. Waite's long list of credentials. Since this same list appears in chapter 5, we have omitted it here.*)

Rex Cobb is the Director of the Baptist Bible Translators Institute. He is a veteran missionary to Mexico. He has taught courses in linguistics since 1973. Probably no one in fundamental Baptist circles has addressed the issues of linguistics and translation as he has. He is fluent in Spanish.

Rex Cobb participated in the translation effort and has endorsed the final product.

H. D. Williams (Dean Burgon Society) has produced a first-class book, *Word for Word Translating of the Received Text, Verbal, Plenary Translating*, on translation principles.

He spent over eight hours with Dr. Gómez, D. A. Waite,

Rex Cobb, Steven Zeinner, myself (I have no idea why I was included in such a group) and others, discussing principles of Bible translation. He has endorsed the RVG based upon the translation principles used.

I have read and heard several critical comments about the RVG by people who question "the scholarship" involved in the project. Yet not one of those men possess any of the qualifications of a scholar, even though some have labeled themselves as such (scholar is not a title you award yourself, nor can it be given to you by a few close friends).

Not a one of them has a fraction of the language credentials of D. A. Waite. None of them have, or could produce a scholarly work on translation or any other subject like those written by D. A. Waite or H. D. Williams.

The critics' academic credentials are slender and their record of scholarly accomplishments non-existent. Few have any record of any ministry accomplishments.

4. I support the RVG because it has convinced honest skeptics.

Allen Johnson (Wings Bearing Precious Seed) and Carlos Donate (missionary to Guatemala) are both close friends. Both preach, teach and write in Spanish. Both are deeply committed to the pure word of God in Spanish. Both were very skeptical of the Gómez project in the beginning.

As the project advanced and they looked at rough drafts, both had to acknowledge that this was a genuine Received Text Bible in Spanish. Carlos Donate became involved in the project, helping to review the final drafts.

5. I support the RVG because of the demand for it.

I have met a number of American missionaries and Hispanic nationals who testify that this project is an answer to prayers they have been praying for a long time.

Dr. Steven Zeinner is a long-time veteran missionary to Mexico, and now director of Bearing Precious Seed, Global. He has told me of seeing hundreds of requests for the RVG in a very short time span.

6. I support the RVG because of its availability.

Anyone can freely print the RVG 2010. The Word of God should not be bound by man. When you print modern Bibles, you have to pay royalties to a modernist Bible Society. But when you print the RVG you don't have to pay a penny to anyone.

7. I support the RVG because it has an honest name.

Throughout the centuries, Bible translations have been identified by the primary editor, translator or sponsor of the translation. This allows people to immediately identify the translation, the text, and the principles behind it.

God has used the Smith-Van Dyke in Arabic, The Tyndale Bible, The Coverdale Bible, The Matthews Bible, The Taverner Bible in English, The Lutheran Bible in German, The Diodati Bible in Italian, The Reina-Valera in Spanish, The Ostervald Bible in French, and The King James Bible in English.

A name which identifies the primary individual behind the translation is an honest name.

8. I support the RVG because of its critics.

The critics who attack the RVG have unknowingly given a great reason to support it. They constantly claim that the RVG matches the readings of the King James Bible. They claim that this is because the gringos pressured Dr. Gómez to bring the English into the Spanish.

Actually, all of the Spanish readings they defend also match English Bibles. These men are comfortable when their Spanish Bible is identical to the Revised Standard Version, the New English Version or even the Jehovah's Witness New World Translation. But they border on hysterical when a Spanish reading matches the King James Bible.

This tells me everything I need to know about these men and also everything I need to know about the Reina-Valera Gómez Bible.

CONCLUSION

I know Humberto Gómez *well*. I don't agree with him about everything, but I don't agree with anyone about everything.

He is a compassionate soul winner. He has been a very effective church planter. He is fearless and he does not bend to political pressure or intimidation. Men that I deeply respect like Dr. Jon Jenkins and Dr. Mickey Carter have endorsed his ministry. God always matches a man with a moment. He has matched Humberto with this moment.

Many Bible colleges, mission boards, and Christian publishing ministries loudly proclaim that they are Received Text based when they are raising money. They now have a chance to prove that they mean it. Just as they have a Received Text Bible to use, support and distribute in English (the King James Bible), they now have a Received Text Bible to use, support and distribute in Spanish.

I was pleased to find out that Chick Publications is now printing and using the RVG. Victory Baptist Press is also printing it. Also, Bible Education and Missionary Service (BEAMS) is distributing it.

Now is the opportunity for the faithful supporters of the Received Text and the King James Bible to stand up and be counted.

CHAPTER 9

Do You Have the Courage to Stand?

Did I fear a great multitude, or did the contempt of families terrify me, that I kept silence, and went not out of the door?[59]

A few years prior to writing this book, a well-known and respected Hispanic pastor of an independent Baptist church invited me out for breakfast at a local restaurant.

This pastor is a man I highly respect for his many years of faithfulness in the ministry. He uses the RV 1960.

During this time of fellowship, this dear pastor expressed his concerns for me in regards to my decision to use the RVG rather than the RV 1960.

---

59) Job 31:34.

For about two hours he tried his best to explain to me why he felt it was a bad idea for me to use the RVG. He predicted trouble in the ministry as a result of my decision. I'll never forget what he told me. He warned:

> Brother Manny, if you continue to stand for the RVG, you will bring a lot of unnecessary grief and heartache upon your family because of those who will oppose you for your position.

Many Christians today claim to stand for a lot of things. But a stand is not a true stand unless there is a price to pay or something to lose. The proof of this can be found in every example in the Bible of someone who took a stand for what he or she believed.

The Spanish Bible issue is no different. The nature of the flesh is to choose the path of least resistance. Many Christians today do no longer know what it is like to take a stand. I believe this is due to the times in which we live.

THE COST OF NO PERSECUTION

Throughout the history of true Bible-believing Christianity, persecution was a normal way of life. Making the choice to be a Christian by faith in the atoning blood of Jesus Christ came with the understanding that you may have to die for that decision. The threat of persecution and death was imminent.

However, for many Christians today, these hazards are the furthest things from their minds. They will never know what it is like to live with the very real threat of horrible persecution that our Christian forefathers lived with on a daily basis.

Because of this, I believe we now have a generation of Christians who have lost the courage to stand up for what is right.

Most Christians today base their decisions on what to believe in or where to "stand" according to whatever position is being espoused by the status quo… or by some Christian celebrity… or by what is believed by the people in their circle of fellowship. They do not have the diligence, conviction, or the audacity to think for themselves and allow God's Word to be the final authority.

> The fear of man bringeth a snare: but whoso putteth his trust in the LORD shall be safe.[60]

We must remind ourselves that, had the Lord caved in to the opposition He faced, we would all be eternally damned, and that without remedy.

May the love of Christ constrain us to remember the praise of David in Psalm 144:1-2:

> Blessed be the LORD my strength, which teacheth my hands to war, and my fingers to fight: My goodness, and my fortress; my high tower, and my deliverer; my shield, and he in whom I trust; who subdueth my people under me.

I have often thought about the warning given to me by that concerned pastor in the restaurant. But the more I

---

60) Proverbs 29:25.

read my Bible, the more I see that the Christian life is full of trouble.

The Bible says that we "must through much tribulation enter into the kingdom of God."[61]

> Many are the afflictions of the righteous.[62]
>
> Yea, and all that will live godly in Christ Jesus shall suffer persecution.[63]

Trouble is inevitable, *especially* if you are in the ministry. So understanding these things, I have decided that if trouble must come, let it come as a result of taking a good stand rather than as a consequence of compromising the truth. Let us endure hardness as good soldiers of Jesus Christ.

> Moreover it is required in stewards, that a man be found faithful.[64]

There will always be opposition. But when the dust settles, may we be able to lay our heads at night on the soft pillow of a clear conscience.

Dearly beloved, I cannot violate my conscience. I must be consistent to what I truly believe with all my heart. As God is my witness, I believe the RVG is the pure Word of God in Spanish.

I have prayed many hours with tears over this issue, seeking the face of God for direction in a tough and controversial issue. I must go with God!

My admonition to you dear reader is to *go with God!*

---

61) Acts 14:22
62) Psalm 34:19.
63) 2 Timothy 3:12.
64) 1 Corinthians 4:2.

It is better to trust in the LORD than to put
confidence in man.[65]

For God has promised:

I will never leave thee, nor forsake thee. So that
we may boldly say, The Lord is my helper, and
I will not fear what man shall do unto me.[66]

Let Him be your guide in this issue, yea, in every other
issue as well. For our God is a God of truth. And no matter
what man does, the truth will prevail. And there is nothing
anyone can do to stop it.

But if it be of God, ye cannot overthrow it; lest
haply ye be found even to fight against God.[67]

In closing, I leave you with the following words of Dr.
Humberto Gómez in the next chapter.

---

65) Psalm 118:8.
66) Hebrews 13:5-6.
67) Acts 5:39.

CHAPTER 10

The Price that was Paid

By Dr. Humberto Gómez

Casiodoro de Reina and Cipriano de Valera paid a great price to give us the Word of God in our Spanish language. We owe a great debt of gratitude to these two champions of the faith.

When Reina, in the early 1500s, learned that salvation comes, not through the church, nor through baptismal regeneration, but by grace through faith in the Lord Jesus Christ, plus nothing and minus nothing, he got gloriously saved.

He immediately left the Catholic church and a passion began to burn in his heart that the entire Spanish speaking world might come to the knowledge of the truth. What better way for the Spanish-speaking world to have access to the truth than to translate the Bible into their language so they could be free.

As we have seen, it took him several years to complete his task. He was persecuted, criticized, and lived a life of pain and sickness. But all that did not stop him from doing his work. He had to work in his own small linen business to provide for his family.

It took almost forty years to sell the first 2600 copies of his Bible. Persecution, sickness, pain, criticism and financial needs were his lot in life. The same can be said of Valera. They both suffered the same things.

Despite the price, the obstacles, and opposition, they remained *settled, strong, sweet*, and *small.*

SETTLED

They remained resolved, resolute, determined, and unwavering in their task.

STRONG

They did not soften their message. Like John the Baptist, they did not tell the king what he *wanted* to hear but what he *needed* to hear.

SWEET

They did not retaliate against their critics. They never became bitter over all they suffered or for the lack of support. To them the support from above was sufficient. They considered their work for the Spanish-speaking world to be a privilege.

SMALL

It never went to their head. Arrogance stops the flow to the brain and oftentimes it stops the oxygen. Cipriano de Valera had to flee Spain from the Catholic Inquisition, and he became the pastor of a small church known as "the Church of the Fugitives."

The driving force of their work was their desire for the common people to have the very Words of life. They wanted them to also find that salvation comes not through the church, nor through baptismal regeneration, but through faith in Christ and faith alone.

It is my prayer that we all will take a stand for the text that God has honored throughout the centuries – the Traditional Texts. We cannot remain idle while we see the Critical Texts dethroning the Textus Receptus before of our very eyes, and that with the complacency and sometimes complicity of the fundamental movement.

Here are the words of another translator, Missionary Bob Patton:

> We are praying that the Lord will raise up an army of fundamental translators using the right text, the right methods, to His glory, and that we should band together as well. Too long we have complained about the evangelicals and liberals translating, but not done the work ourselves. We pray that there will be unity of purpose and a real outpouring of the Lord's blessing on His word and His work.

Some are calling our revision *perfect!* Some are calling it *private* (and everything in between). With humility I can say that, to do this work, we gave ten years of our lives.

With all our heart, mind, and spirit we literally put our ministries, families and reputations on the line. The task was greater than any one could imagine. Countless hours of labor and agonizing prayer are behind this work.

Those who use the RVG testify that they love this Bible. It seems like God has honored it by bringing salvation to many souls, and several churches are being started with the RVG. Deep in my heart I believe that the RVG is the most exact and faithful rendition of the inspired and preserved Word of God, The very Words of God in Spanish.

In Christ,

Dr. Humberto Gómez Sr.

CHAPTER 11

Testimonies and Endorsements

But the word of God grew and multiplied.[68]

THE TESTIMONY OF A
BIBLE PRINTER

By Jim Fellure, director of Victory Baptist Press in Milton, Florida, which prints the RVG Spanish Bible.

For over fifty years the Scofield Reference Bible, first published in 1917 by the Oxford University Press, was the most popular study Bible in existence among fundamental, Bible-believing Christians.

---

68) Acts 12:24.

In 1967 the study notes were revised, but the editors also tampered with the text. They made many critical changes, but the change most often referred to by fundamentalists was Daniel 3:25.

When the three Hebrew children were cast into the furnace of fire, King Nebuchadnezzar looked in and said:

> Lo, I see four men loose, walking in the midst
> of the fire, and they have no hurt; and the form
> of the fourth is like the Son of God.

The 1967 edition of the Scofield Bible changed the words "the Son of God" to "a son of the gods." The critics of our English King James Bible would say that "a son of the gods" was only the description the king gave the fourth man in the fire.

That is a ridiculous view because the gods never had sons, and if they had, their sons would not have had the power to deliver from the fire. Without a doubt, the fourth man in the fire was a pre-incarnate appearance of "the Son of God" not "a son of the gods."

Because of that one critical change, most fundamentalists rejected the New Scofield Reference Bible, and rightly so.

In 1980, Brother Jack Wood showed Brother Humberto Gómez that same verse (Daniel 3:25) in his Spanish Bible. It had the same wording as the New Scofield.

From that time on Brother Gómez began making notes of other errors as he found them and hoping for the day when some qualified person would produce a Spanish Bible that was reliable in all parts and yet maintain the accuracy and beauty of the Spanish language.

Finally, in the year 2000, Brother Gómez dedicated himself to the task. With the help of twenty years worth of personal notes, and many willing contributors, by 2003 all the known errors in the Spanish New Testament had been corrected, and Brother Gómez approached us about printing it.

We spent an entire afternoon having Brother Gómez show us verses in different Spanish Bibles with errors, telling us how he had translated the verses and why he did it.

We were very impressed with what we saw, but I wanted to give it a more thorough test. To be sure of getting a non-prejudiced view, we printed just a few copies and distributed them among other Spanish-speaking Bible believers who did not know Brother Gómez.

Dr. D. A. Waite, president of the Dean Burgeon Society and editor of the Defined King James Bible, was the first person we contacted. Dr. Waite requested ten copies to distribute among people he knew and, after they scrutinized the text, he found one error. It was an oversight on Brother Gómez's part and he immediately corrected the verse.

Dr. Waite has since become a friend of Brother Gómez and a strong supporter of the RVG Spanish Bible.

The second person we contacted was Dr. Rex Cobb of the Bible Translators Institute. Brother Cobb compared 220 verses in eight different Spanish translations and came out with a strong endorsement for the RVG.

Since then men like Dr. Phil Stringer, Dr. Stephen Zeinner, Dr. Micky Carter, and a host of others, including good missionaries too numerous to list, have endorsed the RVG.

Through the many endorsements, we are convinced that the RVG is the best Spanish Bible in existence.

We immediately printed 30,000 New Testaments and 200,000 John/Romans. The Old Testament has now been completed and another printing ministry has already printed 35,000 paperback copies of the whole RVG Bible, and Brother Gómez, at great expense, has had hardback, bonded leather and genuine leather copies printed.

The RVG Spanish Bible, without any major advertisement campaigns, is becoming more popular all the time. There is seldom a day goes by that Victory Baptist Press does not ship several hundred, and some days several thousand of the glue bound, vinyl cover editions to the mission field without charge.

The RVG/KJV, genuine leather bound, English and Spanish parallel is by far the most popular among the different editions of the RVG Bible. The demand for these Bibles is so great that we are considering a distribution center in one of the South, or Central America Spanish speaking countries.

Also, Chick Publications and two tract printing ministries that I know of, have begun using the RVG in all of their Spanish tracts, and I presently know of two other printing or scripture distribution ministries that are considering going to the RVG exclusively.

Dr. Jim Fellure
Victory Baptist Press, Milton, Florida
www.victorybaptistpress.com

THE TESTIMONY OF A NATIVE
MEXICAN PASTOR

By Pastor Ulises Velázquez.

The subject of which Spanish Bible to use is a theme that many are very passionate about and it has brought great controversy to the Fundamental Spanish world. However I believe the time of reconciliation has arrived.

I should say beforehand that it is not my desire to be contentious or rude toward others that use other Bible versions in Spanish. In my Christian life, I have come across many difficult decisions that have required sacrifice and courage to make. The topic of the Bible is no exception.

I have decided to use the Reina-Valera Gómez and I will explain why. I will start by giving some of my testimony.

In 1992, the first time someone told me about Christ, they used the Reina-Valera 1909. I was living in Mexicali, B.C., Mexico. I worked for a company that rented commercial buildings since I had received my title as a Bi-Lingual Administrative Assistant in the city of Durango.

I was saved through this Bible and the first Bible I bought was the 1909, a Bible that is close to my heart even today. However, the first Fundamental Independent Baptist church I went to used the RV 1960. This was the most common Bible, and the one I used most to preach from.

In 1994, I went to a Missions Conference in Santa Catarina, Nuevo León, Mexico and for the first time I witnessed something very unusual. I found brothers in Christ attacking and criticizing the version of the Bible that I used (the Reina-Valera 1960).

This greatly surprised me, and at the time I was very bothered and frustrated by it all. They stood firmly behind the Antigua (Old Version) 1909. They defended it and refuted those that used any other "modern" version.

As time went by, even though I used both Bibles equally, I grew to love the RV 1960 more and more because it used the word "salvation" *(salvación)* instead of "health" *(salud)*, but I always thought there should be a reconciliation between the two.

The word *Hades* was without a doubt something that I never liked in the 1960, especially when I tried to confront the false doctrines of the Jehovah's Witnesses.

When this would happen I found myself "correcting" the RV 1960 Bible that used the word *Hades* and used *infierno* (hell) as the Old Version (1909).

Other controversies like, "curse God and die" *(maldice a Dios)* instead of "bless God and die" *(bendice a Dios)* in the book of Job 2:9, also, "he that washes his clothes" instead of "he that keepeth his commandments" in Revelation 22:14 always bothered me.

In 1996 God called me to preach, and I started an online ministry (www.interbiblia.com).

My dream was to make the Word of God available to the Spanish-speaking world, and have articles and evangelistic material, but I ran into a problem: the Bible I used was copyrighted. Because of that fact, all of my dreams came to a halt.

The only Bible version I could use was the 1909, which was very difficult for me to use and recommend with all of my heart.

There was always a prayer in my heart to have a Bible that would balance both Bibles and be available so that anyone could use and distribute it.

By way of Bible programs like "Theophilos," I studied the Authorized Version in English (the King James Bible) and I noticed that there was also a controversy about the Bible in this language as well.

In 1998 I got my hands on a book entitled *Let's Weigh the Evidence,* published by Chick Publications. Since that time, I started to understand the influence of the devil in the contemporary Bibles in the English language.

While reading the history of the English Bible, I discovered the great difference in how the Bible was brought to the English language. I also noticed the great scholarship of the men involved in that translation.

But when it came to Spanish Bibles, I always noticed the inconsistencies between the RV 1909 and the RV 1960, as well as the older versions.

In 2003, a brother came to the church where I was preaching. He was promoting the modern and corrupt Spanish Bible, *La Biblia de las Américas* or "Bible of America." Now it was my turn to show him why the Reina-Valera Bible was better than that Bible.

I found an article written by Terry Watkins that compared 300 verses from the King James Bible to seven other modern versions.

I decided to use this article to compare those verses in *La Biblia de las Américas* and defend what my Bible said in the Reina-Valera (1909 and 1960).

I was very surprised the moment I started looking at what both Reina-Valera Bibles said. I found verses in both that were affected by the critical manuscripts, though not all the verses.

I finished my article "defending" the Reina-Valera Bible, and it was sufficient to help this person understand our position, and that we couldn't use his Bible.

But without a doubt a dart was stuck in my heart. My eyes were also opened to the need for a Bible without the influence of the Egyptian manuscripts, and gnostics, and that I could defend with a clean conscience.

Finally the brother using the *La Biblia de las Américas* left the church very offended because one of the translators of that Bible was his teacher in seminary and he could not accept that such a scholar could be wrong in his translation of the Bible.

My response was very simple. I told him the problem was not the scholarship of his professor, but rather the text (manuscript) he used for his translation. I also discovered inconsistencies between the Spanish versions of the Bible (1909 and 1960) and the English Bible.

The study I did with *La Biblia de las Américas* opened my eyes to the influence the devil had brought even to the Spanish Bibles.

From there forward I studied about the manuscripts. Spiritually speaking, those who use Bibles that come from the defective Egyptian manuscripts were not content with their spiritual departure, and sent their manuscripts to influence our modern Bibles, and to bring us back under their control little by little.

The series by Brother Thomas Holland was a great help to my life. I learned that using a corrupt base text produces defective Bibles. And I could see that the hand of God was upon the English Bible, and that God had brought revival through it.

There were missionaries who were translating directly from the King James versions into other languages where they didn't have the Word of God, and millions had been saved throughout the world, thanks to the work of the Bible in English.

The subject of the manuscripts is ignored in the majority of the Spanish Bible seminaries, and the devil has taken advantage of this area in the Fundamental circles.

In my personal study I concluded that if we ignore this subject then we have no ground to stand on against the modern corrupted Bible versions in Spanish like the "Reina-Valera Actualizada," "Biblia al Día," "Versión Popular" or other versions that are infested and influenced by the gnostic and Egyptian manuscripts.

Brother Gómez has had a sincere attitude and a great heart for the work of this revision. He has had the backing of men of God who know the original languages, and are experts in translation.

When I found out that the RVG revision of the Bible was not influenced with the Critical Texts, and had been compared to the Authorized Version in English it caught my attention immediately.

With the RVG Bible I see the opportunity to reconcile fundamentalism in Spanish with the fundamentalism in English. With the RVG Bible, I see the opportunity to have our Bible printed in our print shops and freely distributed.

In the RVG Bible I see a Bible that reconciled the Reina-Valera Bibles with the Received Text and Masoretic Text, as well as the Authorized Version in English.

This is a Bible without the influence of corrupt Egyptian manuscripts and the gnostic texts that have become so prominent in our world today.

Brethren, I encourage you to study the diabolic influences in our modern Bibles for yourself. It is time for us to unite in the battle against Bibles that have been affected by the enemy.

Not one single verse in the Reina-Valera Gómez has been affected by corrupt manuscripts. In its entirety, it is the Word of God. Read it, study it, and discover it for yourself.

We must unite at once, Spanish-speaking Christians as well as English speaking Christians, in our labor to reach the world with the Gospel of our Lord Jesus Christ.

Your servant in Christ,
Missionary Ulises Velázquez
Editor of Interbiblia
www.interbiblia.com

· · · · · · · · · ·

AN ENDORSEMENT BY TODAY'S PREMIER DEFENDER OF THE RECEIVED TEXTS

By Dr. D. A. Waite

I am pleased to recommend the Spanish Bible of Dr. Humberto Gómez. I have found him to be a kind, careful, humble, and able student who has spent hundreds of hours in carrying out his burden to get the Spanish Bible of 1909 (by which he was led to the Lord Jesus Christ as his Saviour) in line with the Hebrew, Aramaic, and Greek Words underlying the King James Bible.

He has done this. He spoke with me about several questions he had in certain places of his translation in an effort to be both clear and correct.

He did an excellent job when he spoke at our Dean Burgon Society in 2005 concerning the need for an accurate Spanish Bible.

He sought to correct the various errors of translation in both the Old and New Testaments. His Spanish New Testament followed the Greek Received or Traditional Text on which the King James Bible was based.

Most of the other Spanish Bibles, such as the 1960 and even the 1909, have followed in whole or in part the false Westcott and Hort Critical Greek Text that gives an erroneous and doctrinally incorrect reading.

There are over 8,000 documented differences between the Received Greek Texts and the Revised Critical Greek Texts. Included in these 8,000 differences are at least 356

doctrinal passages where the Revised Greek Text is in doctrinal error. I have listed 158 of the more important of these
356 doctrinal passages in Chapter V of my book, *Defending
the King James Bible.*

I have personally looked up in Dr. Humberto Gómez's
Spanish Bible each one of those 158 passages in my book. I
found every one of them to be in conformity to the Received
Greek Text and have been made doctrinally correct. This
cannot be said of the RV 1960 and even the RV 1909 in
each of these places.

Dr. Gómez also corrected some of the places where there
are translational errors in the other Spanish Bibles such as
in Psalm 12:6-7; Exodus 25:18, 19, 20, 21,22; John 3:5;
Matthew 4:3; Matthew 26:63, and in other places both in
the Old and New Testaments.

Dr. Gómez knew that there might be places in his translation where further correction would be needed, and he was
humble enough and honest enough to welcome suggestions
in this regard from whatever quarters.

When such suggestions were received, Dr. Gómez weighed
them carefully, and if he felt they had merit, he made the
changes in his next printing. Could any Spanish-speaking
person wish for more?

Though I know and speak Spanish fairly well, I would
never attempt to translate the Spanish Bible. Dr. Gómez,
on the other hand, has that language as his native tongue,
and knows the fine differences and shades of the meanings
of words that non-native speakers cannot know.

May the Lord Jesus Christ our Saviour bless the efforts

of this humble servant of God who is trying to get into the hands of his Spanish-speaking friends the Words of God in Spanish just like we have in our King James Bible the Words of God in English. This indeed is a noble and needed task.

Sincerely for God's Words,

Pastor D. A. Waite, Th.D., Ph.D.

Bible For Today Baptist Church

• • • • • • • • • • •

THE ADMONITION OF VETERAN BIBLE TRANSLATOR

I began using a Spanish Bible in 1976. I chose to use the Antigua Version of 1909. Somehow I knew it was a more pure Bible than the only other choice I knew of, the Revision of 1960. I did find, however, some textual problems with the 1909 that were troubling to me as a believer in our Authorized English Bible.

As I ministered in Bible translation, evangelism, church building and Bible institute ministry, I spent literally hundreds, maybe thousands, of hours studying the purity of Spanish Bible versions.

I developed a checklist of 1,100 places in the New Testament where there are differences between the Received Text and the Critical Text. (My list is small compared to the list by Mr. Jack Moorman. He lists 8,000 differences.)

I then compared sixteen different Spanish New Testaments against this list. I discovered that there is a big difference between corrupt Critical Text Bibles and those coming from the Received Text.

I did find that, beginning about the time that Westcott and Hort were doing their devilment on the English Bible (about 1862), some began making changes in the Reina-Valera Bible to move it toward the Critical Text.

The Bible I used contained several of these Critical Text changes, but I found that the revisers of the 1960 revision added many more Critical Text readings to the Reina-Valera.

Also during those days I began to pray that God would give us a good, faithful revision of the Reina-Valera that would be equivalent to my English Bible. Of course, I did not want a literal King James Bible in Spanish. That is not possible. The KJV is an English Bible.

A few years ago I learned about the work of Humberto Gómez and became very interested. When I finally received a copy of his initial work, I liked it, but found a few things that could use a little work. I only found one small textual problem, and Brother Gómez promptly corrected that.

Over the next few years we communicated from time to time about improvements to his work. He was always happy to listen to any suggestion I had. He didn't always follow them, but he always gave a good explanation as to why he couldn't.

During those years Brother Gómez was open to suggestions from all the Spanish-speaking brethren. In 2008 I read completely through the RVG Bible. I liked the way it read and believe it to be good Spanish.

I would encourage anyone who cares about Bible purity to seriously consider using this Bible. I would especially encourage local church Bible-printing ministries that stand for pure Bibles to print this RVG Spanish Bible.

For those who do not want to change from the Bible they currently use, I understand that it is difficult to tell people that there are problems in their Bible. The easy thing to do is to pretend that these Critical Text problems do not exist. Personally, I cannot accept a Bible with a considerable number of corruptions. If others can, that is between them and God.

I would urge missionaries in Spanish-speaking countries, however, to be candid with the pastors in the U.S. who ask which Spanish Bible they use. It is going to be very difficult in the days to come to say, "The Bible I use (referring to the 1960) is just like the King James." The pastors in the States are going to know this simply is not true.

We make a big deal about the English Bible; and I think we should. But are we consistent to be so "strong" on the KJV in English and so "weak" when it comes to Bibles in other languages, such as Spanish? May God help us drop our politics and loyalties to friends and fellowships, and be true to God and His pure word.

We must also consider what is best for the Spanish-speaking people to whom God has called us. Are we English speakers better than they? Do we somehow deserve a perfect Bible, but Spanish speakers don't?

Yours for the pure word of God,
Rex L. Cobb,
rexcobb@juno.com

• • • • • • • • • •

MORE TESTIMONIES FROM
AROUND THE WORLD

For the Spanish speaking world, our God has provided for us in majestic Castilian Spanish the Textus Receptus-based revision of the Reina-Valera 1909 —the Reina-Valera Gómez 2010 or RVG.

Since the first edition came off the presses in 2004, this Bible has caused a sensation among many people, both Spanish speakers and English-speaking missionaries to the Hispanics.

It has undergone several improvements since its debut, each time improving the text, and lining it up beautifully with the Textus Receptus and the King James Version.

For those of us who longed and prayed for a Spanish Bible that is faithful to the God-honored Textus Receptus, as well as the beloved King James (or Authorized Version), that time has come.

Allow me to share with you three reasons why all Bible-believing Christians should share the responsibility to stand for and promote the Reina-Valera Gómez Bible.

The most important reason is because of the *purity* of the RVG compared to Bibles containing corrupt, Critical Text material. The sinlessness, work, and Deity of our Lord Jesus Christ, along with vital doctrines such as the virgin birth, salvation by grace, sanctification, separation, hell, etc. are all upheld, and God is thereby glorified.

Bibles containing Critical Texts which cause changes

or omissions that attack our fundamental doctrines do not glorify God, cannot be trusted and must be rejected.

Second, the *availability* of the RVG 2010. Even though it is copyrighted, anyone can freely print it, provided they don't change any of the text. The copyright's purpose is to protect the text from Bible corrupters.

Third, the Spanish-speaking Christians are now "without excuse." We have a pure copy of the Word of God. For many years the only choice for the Bible in Spanish was the RV 1909 and the RV 1960, both of which have been watered down and mutilated by modernistic translators, (the RV 1960 especially). Now a pure Bible in Spanish is available to all, and there is now no excuse!

For God's pure Words,
Joseph Martinez
Missionary to Hispanics, and veteran church planter

• • • • • • • • • •

Everything started when I read the book *The Transmission Of The Text Of The New Testament And Our Bibles Of Today* by Rudulf Ebertehäuser. For years I used the RV 1960 and was very content, but when I read this book I learned that the 1960 does not follow the Textus Receptus faithfully. Some verses lean upon the Critical Text.

I asked myself, "How is it possible that for years no one has told me anything?" I have been in different churches yet no one has ever said anything to me on this subject.

I searched the internet and found websites referring to this subject. First, I enquired about the RV 1909 and even though it is more faithful than the RV 1960, I found words difficult to comprehend because of their antiquity.

I continued searching and I was sent an RV 1865. I liked this version very much because it was more faithful to the Received Text, but it also had antiquated Castilian words.

I consulted about this with brethren in other churches and they told me that, for the time being, there were no other revisions.

I continued searching and found another revision edited in Columbia, the SEVA. I contacted them to get a Bible but they told me that it was too expensive to send by mail.

I searched one more time and finally found the RVG on the website, www.rices4peru.com.

I downloaded the RVG Bible and compared with e-sword several well-known verses that the RV 1960 changed, like Luke 2:22, Daniel 3:25, 2 Kings 10:25, I Corinthians 10:9, Hebrews 10:34 and many others.

In what I have been able to prove, the RVG follows the Textus Receptus faithfully. We Spanish-speaking Christians were in need of a Bible faithful to the Castilian.

Vicente Martin Delgado, Spain

• • • • • • • • • •

We have used the RVG in our churches and Bible Institute for more than two years. We have found it to be the most accurate translation available in Spanish... I am proud to endorse the revision by Brother Gómez.

Tim Urling
Missionary in Mexico
www.2EveryCreature.com

· · · · · · · · · · ·

In recent days, there is a Reina-Valera Gómez Spanish Bible. Humberto Gómez has carefully aligned the 1909 Reina-Valera with the King James text. Reports coming to me indicate that the RVG is getting strong support and wide acceptance among the Spanish brethren.

Dr. Shelton Smith
Editor, Sword of the Lord
www.swordofthelord.com

· · · · · · · · · · ·

It is a privilege to be the first missionary outside of the continental US to receive and use the Reina-Valera Gómez Bible. I pray that many others will see the benefits of this Bible and begin using it in their ministry.

Don Rich
Missionary in Peru
www.rich2peru.com

· · · · · · · · · · ·

Soon after being saved in 1983 I had the blessing of going to an Independent Baptist Fellowship meeting where I was first made aware that there was not an accurate Spanish Bible. This fact is not a mystery to anyone.

For seventeen years I have compared Spanish Bibles, looking for an accurate version where I didn't have to apologize or explain away obvious errors.

For over two years, I have had the blessing of having in my hand the Reina-Valera Gómez and can now state, without a doubt, that we have an accurate and reliable Bible in Spanish likened unto the KJV.

Joe A. Martinez
Missionary in Argentina

• • • • • • • • • •

In 1993, after earning my master's of education degree in linguistics at Baptist Bible Translators, and learning Spanish in 1995, I became thoroughly immersed in language learning and the study of the Spanish Bible conflict as a missionary in Chile.

And after these many years of looking for a textually pure Spanish Bible that agrees with the Masoretic Hebrew Text, the Textus Receptus Greek Text, and our revered King James Bible, we have found it in the Reina-Valera Gómez Bible.

This Bible represents a revival of old-time convictions in bibliology that have been lost by the average Hispanic believer and pastor during the 1909 and 1960 revisions.

But now we can say that the church is recapturing the spirit of Cipriano de Valera of 1602 when he said:

> I implore God by his infinite mercy that He inspire in the heart of the King that he mandate at his cost the gathering of pious and knowledgeable men in the Hebrew and Greek tongues that they review this translation of the Bible; whom with a sincere and pious desire, that desire to serve God and do good to their nation, that they compare and challenge it with the Hebrew text that God dictated to his holy prophets before the coming of Christ, and with the Greek text that he himself dictated to his holy Apostles and Evangelists after the coming of Christ in the flesh.[69]

Obviously, the time of the king is long past. But the desire of Valera has been faithfully continued in the Reina-Valera Gómez Bible, and it is a wonderful work. We will be using it as our Standard in our Spanish ministries.

Donald Heinz
Missionary in Chile
www.palabraspuras.wordpress.com

• • • • • • • • • •

I have polled many Hispanic preachers around the

---

69) Exhortation to the Reader, Valera 1602 Bible.

world who welcome the RVG 2010 with open arms. Brother Gómez spoke before a congress of Hispanic fundamentalist leaders from the USA, Mexico, Central and South America, representing not just Baptists, but old-time Methodists, Missionary Alliance, Bible Presbyterian, and Bible churches as well.

This group has stood firmly for the 1909 Antigua ever since United Bible Society began promoting Westcott and Hort in the early 1950s.

After the first presentation was given by Dr. Gómez, the reaction was one of caution, but as the week progressed, the delegates had an opportunity to compare verses from RVG (2nd edition) and the 1909. The overwhelming approval and support for the RVG was made known to all by the group's leader. Also, the leading Christian radio station in Guatemala has publicly endorsed it, and is promoting it daily.

Carlos Donate
Missionary in Guatemala

• • • • • • • • • •

I stand for the perfect and preserved words of the KJV and the RVG. Let me tell you, It is *perfect!* I praise the Lord for what He has done, giving me His perfect words in Spanish!

Nelson Giménez
Pastor in Paraguay
www.relacionconcristopy.blogspot.com

• • • • • • • • • •

We have elected to use the newly published revision of the 1909 Bible produced by Brother Humberto Gómez. We are using it in the John and Romans edition that we pass out, as well as for preaching and public reading. Since the middle of August we have seen some 28 people saved.

We are thankful for a Bible that is faithful to the Received Text and praise the Lord for the good reception it has had so far.

Elson Portugal
Missionary to Costa Rica

• • • • • • • • • •

I strongly recommend the Gómez edition, both the Spanish and the parallel King James edition. I believe the Gómez edition is the best work we have today in matching the King James Bible. I also see the hand of God upon it as it is being accepted so rapidly everywhere.

I also appreciate the good, humble spirit of Brother Humberto Gómez, the man that God is using as His instrument in doing this needed work.

If you have any question, I suggest an honest comparison of the Bibles. If you accept the King James Bible as God's standard to measure by, you will be pleased.

Dr. Mickey Carter
Landmark Baptist Church, Haines City, Florida
President of Landmark Baptist College

• • • • • • • • • •

I have been a missionary in Peru since 2002. I have, with great interest, studied the matter of the Spanish Bible since arriving in Peru. I firmly believe that one day I will stand before Almighty God and give an account for my decisions in the ministry as well as my personal life.

I have read every book I could get my hands on. I have done in-depth studies and comparisons of many Spanish Bibles. I have studied the history of the Spanish Bible and firmly believe that the RVG 2010 is the most accurate and best Bible for the Spanish-speaking world.

The beauty and purity of the Spanish language has been maintained, as well as a strict adherence to the Textus Receptus and Masoretic texts that the King James Bible is based on. Please visit my website to see some charts I have put together: www.rices4peru.com.

Shane D. Rice
Missionary in Peru

• • • • • • • • • •

It has been demonstrated to our satisfaction that every mistake we have ever been shown in any of the Spanish versions has been corrected in the RVG revision. It is our prayer that the Lord would sanction this revision with a great revival throughout the Hispanic world.

Pastor Tim Fellure
Victory Baptist Church, Milton, Florida
www.vbcmilton.org

• • • • • • • • • •

I was using the 1865 Spanish Bible until I found many errors. I did not have peace in my heart using this Bible. The 1865 really attacks the word "hell" (*infierno*) in the Old Testament... I studied this issue every day for more than two years. I am convinced that the RVG is the Word of God for the Spanish-speaking people. It has never been easier to win souls to Christ.

The Holy Spirit is testifying to this Bible. The Christians here are accepting the RVG as the Word of God. They read it, believe it, and love it. Amen, Glory to God!

Mike Wilps
Missionary in Paraguay
www.paraguayforchrist.com

• • • • • • • • • •

We are so grateful to the Lord for giving us a Bible in Spanish that is free from the Critical Texts. While at Bob Jones University I learned and studied about the different manuscripts and where they came from. I leaned heavily in favor of the corrupt Westcott and Hort Greek Texts, and defended the NASV.

When I dropped out of graduate school I soon became aware of my need to search out the other side of this issue. Through personal studies and much help from godly brethren I realized that I was in error and began to rethink my position on the Bible. I am now a firm believer that God has preserved His Word through the Textus Receptus and the Masoretic Text.

As a missionary to Mexico, I was seeking for a Bible that lined up with the pure texts that God has preserved. The RVG meets this criteria more than any other Spanish Bible in the world.

We appreciate the time and sacrifice that Dr. Humberto Gómez put into making this a reality. We know very well that this tremendous work would have never been accomplished without the hand of the Lord.

We highly recommend this precious and pure Bible to anybody. You will love it and appreciate it as you read the Words of God in Spanish with confidence knowing that you are reading a Bible that lines up with the pure and preserved manuscripts, the same that underlies our precious KJV.

Reynaldo Villarreal
Missionary in Mexico

• • • • • • • • • •

I have been a missionary to the country of Chile since 1993. When I first arrived, I followed the lead of veteran missionaries and the already established independent Baptist churches and used the RV 1960.

But after seven years of diligent study I became convinced that the RV 1960 was not the pure Word of God in Spanish, departing from the Hebrew Masoretic Text and the Textus Receptus in literally hundreds of places. Sadly, at that point there was nothing available in print that we could hold up as the pure Word of God in Spanish.

We were anxiously waiting and praying and seeking the Lord's will with regards to the Spanish text. For that past nine years we have traveled many miles and accumulated thousands of pages of materials on the subject.

Then a good friend and co-laborer in the Lord introduced me to the Reina-Valera Gómez. After several years of study and diligent comparisons with the Textus Receptus/KJV, I can say unequivocally that we now have in the RVG a pure Spanish Bible!

We now unashamedly preach from it and promote it in our ministry in the country of Chile and around the world. The price is worth paying, whatever that may be.

Brother Gómez, thank you and keep up the good fight for the faith.

> Gary Castner
> Missionary in Chile

• • • • • • • • • •

I bought a Bible with the King James English on one page and the Reina-Valera 1960 on the other page. I very quickly started finding NIV-type readings in the Spanish.

I next ordered a 1909 Reina-Valera, but after checking a few proof texts, I found some of the same NIV-type readings.

I eventually ordered an 1865 Reina-Valera, but there were

still many readings in this Bible that I did not agree with.

Then, a few months ago, I discovered the RVG. I checked verse after verse after verse, and I must say that I breathed a sigh of relief as I found what I believe to be the closest Spanish Bible to the King James.

Robert W. Thurman
Predicando La Verdad Ministries
Cleveland, Tennessee

• • • • • • • • • •

In the past, I used the Reina-Valera 1960. I did not know anything about the Spanish Bible situation. At that time I did not read the Bible in Spanish. I just used it to go soul winning.

As time went on, I believed the Reina-Valera 1960 to be the Word of God in Spanish. Had I read it completely at that time? No. Had I studied the Bible to know the details about it? No.

My family and I started deputation to go to Mexico as missionaries. We came in contact with many different people and churches. I always defended the 1960 against any other Spanish Bible. I often would get upset at people that used other Spanish versions. They thought that they had the answer and I knew that I had the answer!

After deputation, we arrived in Zacatecas, Mexico and I studied Spanish. I began to read the Spanish Bible, and I studied to preach in Spanish. I preached four times a week.

I had a Spanish Bible program on my computer. It only had the Reina-Valera 1909 and the KJV, so I would copy and paste the 1909 Bible verses to my messages and then open my 1960 and make all the changes so it was right.

I began to notice things that were not right. I had never seen what I was seeing. It did not take long for me to make a change. Our church flyers for the opening day were printed with 1960 Bible verses. Notwithstanding, from the very first day of the church we used the Reina-Valera 1909.

Many people I came in contact with asked me questions about this issue. I began to study and investigate on the differences between the 1909 and the 1960 to be able to answer. As a result of that study I was stronger behind the 1909.

I also saw some things in the 1909 that were not right, but what could I do? We used the Reina-Valera 1909 from August 1999 to August 2007. In church we did a study concerning the bad changes in the 1909 and 1960. We saw from the three Spanish Bibles the differences in the words.

Since August 2007 we have been using the RVG. I believe it is the Word of God in Spanish.

I would love to see the Spanish-speaking people investigate this situation in detail to understand the differences and what Spanish Bible is best. I hope that they will not be as difficult as I was (and am).

Michael Lemma
Missionary in Mexico

• • • • • • • • • •

We are pleased to now offer the Reina-Valera Gómez Bible that has been called, "The most accurate Spanish Bible available" by such organizations as Chick Publications and The Bible For Today/Dean Burgon Society. It is worth noting that all Spanish tracts produced by Chick Publications that once quoted the RV 1960 are now being produced with the RVG 2010. For this reason, we now make the Reina-Valera Gómez an available Spanish Bible option for our customers.

The KJV Store

www.thekjvstore.com

• • • • • • • • • •

The Reina-Valera Gómez Bible is, in our opinion, the best Bible available in the Spanish language at the present time. The Trinitarian Bible Society views the work of Dr. Gómez as most admirable, and we applaud his efforts to provide the Hispanic world with a better Bible than that which had been previously available.

The Trinitarian Bible Society

APPENDIX A

Spanish Bible Verse Comparisons

The chart beginning on the following page was compiled by Michael Lemma. It documents many of the important differences between the various Spanish Bible versions and demonstrates the purity and accuracy of the RVG text.

KJV = King James Version
RVG = Reina-Valera Gómez Bible 2010
LBA = Bible of the Americas 1986
1865 = Valera 1865 revision
1960 = Reina-Valera 1960 revision
NVI = New International Version 1999

	KJV	RVG	LBA	1865	1909	1960	NVI
1 Daniel 3:25 and the form of the fourth is like **the Son of God.**		al Hijo de Dios. ····· the Son of God.	un hijo de los dioses. ····· a son of the gods.	hijo de Dios. ····· a son of God.	hijo de los dioses. ····· a son of the gods.	hijo de los dioses. ····· a son of the gods.	un dios! ····· a god!
Translation is...		**Good**	**Bad**	**Bad**	**Bad**	**Bad**	**Bad**

Jesus is "the Son of God," not "a son of the gods" or "a son of God." Even when unbelievers in the Bible used God's name, it is capitalized.

	KJV	RVG	LBA	1865	1909	1960	NVI
2 Daniel 7:13 *one* like **the Son of man** came		el Hijo del Hombre ····· the Son of Man	un Hijo de Hombre ····· a Son of Man	un Hijo de hombre ····· a Son of man	un hijo de hombre ····· a son of man	un hijo de hombre ····· a son of man	alguien con aspecto humano ····· someone with a human aspect
Translation is...		**Good**	**Bad**	**Bad**	**Bad**	**Bad**	**Bad**

"The Son of Man" means there is just one Son of Man. "A Son of man" means Jesus is one of many sons. Also, the "s" in "Son" should be capitalized.

	KJV	RVG	LBA	1865	1909	1960	NVI
3	2 Chron. 26:18 neither *shall it* be for thine honour from the LORD God.	delante de Jehová Dios. ..... before Jehovah God.	del SEÑOR Dios. ..... of the LORD God.	delante del Dios Jehová. ..... before the God Jehovah.	delante del Dios Jehová. ..... before the God Jehovah.	delante de Jehová Dios. ..... before Jehovah God.	Dios el SEÑOR ..... God the LORD
Translation is...	Good	Good	Good	Bad	Bad	Good	Good

In Spanish, the words: "before the God Jehovah" mean that He is one of many gods.

	KJV	RVG	LBA	1865	1909	1960	NVI
4	Ezra 6:8 for the building of **this house** of God:	esta casa de Dios ..... **this house** of God	esta casa de Dios ..... **this house** of God	la casa de **este Dios** ..... the house of **this God**	la casa de **este Dios** ..... the house of **this God**	esa casa de Dios ..... **that house** of God	la reconstrucción del templo ..... reconstruction of the temple
Translation is...	Good	Good	Good	Bad	Bad	Good	Bad

"This (or that) house of God" refers to the house, not to God. "The house of this God" means that He is one of many gods.

	KJV	RVG	LBA	1865	1909	1960	NVI
5 Isaiah 42:5	Thus saith **God the LORD**	Así dice **Jehová Dios** ..... Thus saith **Jehovah God**	Así dice **Dios el SEÑOR** ..... Thus saith **God the LORD**	Así dice **el Dios Jehová** ..... Thus saith **the God Jehovah**	Así dice **el Dios Jehová** ..... Thus saith **the God Jehovah**	Así dice **Jehová Dios** ..... Thus saith **Jehovah God**	Así dice **Dios, el SEÑOR** ..... Thus saith **God, the LORD**
Translation is...	Good	Good	Good	Bad	Bad	Good	Good

The words "the God Jehovah" mean that He is one of many gods.

	KJV	RVG	LBA	1865	1909	1960	NVI
6 John 12:47 And if any man hear my words, and **believe** not	And if any man hear my words, and **believe** not	no **cree** ..... **believe** not	no las **guarda** ..... does not **keep** them	no las **creyere** ..... **believes** them not	no las **creyere** ..... **believes** them not	no las **guarda** ..... does not **keep** them	no las **obedece** ..... does not **obey** them
Translation is...	Good	Good	Bad	Good	Good	Bad	Bad

The Greek word is "believe," which requires faith. "Keep" and "obey" require works, which can never save.

	KJV	RVG	LBA	1865	1909	1960	NVI
7	Romans 11:30a ye in times past **have not believed** God	no creísteis ····· ye did not believe	fuisteis desobedientes ····· ye were disobedient	no creísteis ····· ye did not believe	no creísteis ····· ye did not believe	erais desobedientes ····· ye were disobedient	fueron desobedientes ····· ye were disobedient
Translation is...	Good	Good	Bad	Good	Good	Bad	Bad

The Greek says "ye have not believed." But some translators changed it to "ye were disobedient," changing the requirement from faith to works.

	KJV	RVG	LBA	1865	1909	1960	NVI
8	Romans 11:30b ...yet have now obtained mercy through their **unbelief**	por la **incredulidad** de ellos ····· through their **unbelief.**	por razón de la **desobediencia** de ellos ····· by reason of their **disobedience.**	por ocasión de la **incredulidad** de ellos ····· by occasion of their **unbelief.**	por la **incredulidad** de ellos ····· through their **unbelief.**	por la **desobediencia** de ellos ····· through their **disobedience.**	por la **desobediencia** de los israelitas ····· through the **disobedience** of the Israelites
Translation is...	Good	Good	Bad	Good	Good	Bad	Bad

	KJV	RVG	LBA	1865	1909	1960	NVI
9 Romans 11:31 Even so have these also now **not believed**	no han creído ····· have not believed	han sido desobedientes ····· have been disobedient	no han creído ····· have not believed	no han creído ····· have not believed	han sido desobedientes ····· have been disobedient	han desobedecido ····· have disobeyed
Translation is...	Good	Bad	Good	Good	Bad	Bad

Changing "not believed" to "disobedient" changes salvation by faith to salvation by obedience (works), a complete heresy.

	KJV	RVG	LBA	1865	1909	1960	NVI
10 Romans 11:32 For God hath concluded them all in **unbelief**	todos en incredulidad ····· all in unbelief	todos en desobediencia ····· all in disobedience	todos en incredulidad all in unbelief	todos en incredulidad ····· all in unbelief	todos en desobediencia ····· all in disobedience	todos a la desobediencia ····· all to the disobedience
Translation is...	Good	Good	Bad	Good	Good	Bad	Bad

	KJV	RVG	LBA	1865	1909	1960	NVI
11	Hebrews 3:18 ...they should not enter into his rest, but to them that **believed not?**	a aquellos que **no creyeron?** ..... them that **believed not?**	a los que **fueron desobedientes?** ..... the ones that **were disobedient?**	a aquellos que **no creyeron?** ..... them that **believed not?**	á aquellos que **no obedecieron?** ..... them that **obeyed not?**	a aquellos que **desobedecieron?** ..... them that **disobeyed?**	a los que **desobedecieron?** ..... the ones that **disobeyed?**
	Translation is...						
	Good	**Good**	**Bad**	**Good**	**Bad**	**Bad**	**Bad**

The correct translation is "believed not." The Jews did not enter into His rest because they did not believe his promise, not because of disobedience. Again, faith is changed to works.

	KJV	RVG	LBA	1865	1909	1960	NVI
12	Hebrews 11:31 By faith the harlot Rahab perished not with them that **believed not**	con los **incrédulos** ..... with the **unbelievers**	con los **desobedientes** ..... with the **disobedient**	con los **incrédulos** ..... with the **unbelievers**	con los **incrédulos** ..... with the **unbelievers**	con los **desobedientes** ..... with the **disobedient**	con los **desobedientes** ..... with the **disobedient**
	Translation is...						
	Good	**Good**	**Bad**	**Good**	**Good**	**Bad**	**Bad**

KJV	RVG	LBA	1865	1909	1960	NVI
13						
Matthew 17:20 Because of your **unbelief**:	Por vuestra **incredulidad** ..... Because of your **unbelief**	Por vuestra **poca fe** ..... Because of your **little faith**	Por vuestra **infidelidad** ..... Because of your **unfaithfulness**	Por vuestra **incredulidad** ..... Because of your **unbelief**	Por vuestra **poca fe** ..... Because of your **little faith**	Porque ustedes tienen tan **poca fe** ..... Because you have **so little faith**
Translation is...						
Good	**Good**	**Bad**	**Bad**	**Good**	**Bad**	**Bad**

The Greek word means "unbelief." "Little faith" is completely wrong, and "unfaithfulness" changes it from faith to works.

KJV	RVG	LBA	1865	1909	1960	NVI
14						
Luke 2:22 of **her** purification	la purificación **de ella** ..... **her** purification	la purificación **de ellos** ..... **their** purification	la purificación **de María** ..... **Mary's** purification	la purificación **de ella** ..... **her** purification	la purificación **de ellos** ..... **their** purification	**ellos debían purificarse** ..... **They should be purified/purify themselves**
Translation is...						
Good	**Good**	**Bad**	**Bad**	**Good**	**Bad**	**Bad**

According to Old Testament law, Mary needed to be purified. But Jesus did not because He never sinned. By saying that Jesus needed to be purified, the 1960 is saying that Jesus was a sinner.

	KJV	RVG	LBA	1865	1909	1960	NVI
15	Matt. 1:23 a virgin shall be with child	una virgen ..... a virgin	la virgen ..... the virgin	una virgen ..... a virgin	la virgen ..... the virgin	una virgen ..... a virgin	La virgen ..... The virgin
	Translation is...						
	Good	Good	Bad	Good	Bad	Good	Bad

"The virgin" is Roman Catholic, exalting Mary as "the forever virgin." "A virgin" is correct because Mary was not a virgin her whole life.

	KJV	RVG	LBA	1865	1909	1960	NVI
16	Isaiah 7:14 a virgin shall conceive,	una virgen ..... a virgin	una virgen ..... a virgin	LA VÍRGEN ..... THE VIRGIN	la virgen ..... the virgin	la virgen ..... the virgin	La joven ..... The young woman
	Translation is...						
	Good	Good	Good	Bad	Bad	Bad	Bad

	KJV	RVG	LBA	1865	1909	1960	NVI
17	Isaiah 58:13 and shalt honour	honrares ..... honours	honras ..... honors	venerares ..... venerates or worships	venerares ..... venerates or worships	venerares ..... venerates or worships	"honorable" ..... "honorable"
	Translation is...						
	Good	Good	Good	Bad	Bad	Bad	Good

The word "venerate" has an unbiblical Roman Catholic meaning. God commanded the Jews to "honor," not "venerate" the Sabbath.

	KJV	RVG	LBA	1865	1909	1960	NVI
18 Matt. 5:22	whosoever is angry with his brother **without a cause**	que **sin razón** se enojare ····· **without a cause** gets angry	aquel que esté enojado ····· is angry	que se enojare **sin razón** ····· gets angry **without a cause**	que se enojare **locamente** ····· gets angry **crazily**	que se enoje ····· gets angry	el que se enoje ····· is angry
Translation is...	**Good**	**Good**	**Bad**	**Good**	**Good**	**Bad**	**Bad**

The words "without a cause" appear in the Greek. By dropping them, the 1960 says that Jesus sinned when he got angry.

	KJV	RVG	LBA	1865	1909	1960	NVI
19 Luke 5:17	the power of the Lord **was** *present* to heal them.	poder del Señor estaba allí para sanarlos. ····· the power of the Lord **was there**	poder del Señor **estaba con Él** para sanar. ····· the power of the Lord **was (temporarily) with him**	virtud del Señor estaba allí para sanarlos. ····· the virtue of the Lord **was there**	virtud del Señor estaba allí para sanarlos. ····· the virtue of the Lord **was there**	poder del Señor **estaba con él** para sanar. ····· the power of the Lord **was (temporarily) with him**	poder del Señor **estaba con él** para sanar a los enfermos. ····· the power of the Lord **was (temporarily) with him**
Translation is...	**Good**	**Good**	**Bad**	**Good**	**Good**	**Bad**	**Bad**

The Lord's power to heal never ended. This is a bad translation and bad doctrine.

	KJV	RVG	LBA	1865	1909	1960	NVI
20	2 Corinthians 5:21 For he hath made **him** *to be* sin for us	lo hizo pecado por nosotros ..... he was made sin for us	le hizo pecado por nosotros ..... he was made sin for us	hizo pecado por nosotros ..... was made sin (or did sin) for us	hizo pecado por nosotros ..... was made sin (or did sin) for us	lo hizo pecado, ... he was made sin	Dios lo trató como pecador ..... God treated him as a sinner
Translation is...	Good	Good	Good	Bad	Bad	Good	Bad

Removing the pronoun "lo" in Spanish, completely changes the meaning. With "lo" it means "He was made sin." Without "lo" it can mean "He did sin." The NVI reading, "God treated him as a sinner," is an interpretation and not a translation.

	KJV	RVG	LBA	1865	1909	1960	NVI
21	Colossians 1:16 For **by him** were all things created,	por Él ..... by Him	en Él ..... in him	en él ..... in him	por él ..... by him	en él ..... in him	por medio de él ..... through him
Translation is...	Good	Good	Bad	Bad	Good	Bad	Bad

All things were created "by" Jesus, the Creator, not "in" Jesus. Jesus didn't create inside Himself. Creation is not part of Himself. Nor was He an instrument that God created "through."

KJV	RVG	LBA	1865	1909	1960	NVI
22 Philippians 2:6 Who, being in the form of God, **thought it not robbery to be equal with God:**	**no tuvo por usurpación** el ser igual a Dios ..... **did not count it as usurpation** being equal with God	**no consideró** el ser igual a Dios **como algo a qué aferrarse** ..... **did not consider** being equal with God as a thing to persist obstinately about	**no tuvo por rapiña** ser igual a Dios ..... **did not count it as plundering** being equal with God	**no tuvo por usurpación** ser igual á Dios: ..... **did not count it as usurpation** being equal with God	**no estimó** el ser igual a Dios **como cosa a qué aferrarse** ..... **did not esteem** being equal with God as a thing to persist obstinately about	**no consideró** el ser igual a Dios **como algo a qué aferrarse** ..... **did not consider** being equal with God as a thing to persist obstinately about
Translation is... **Good**	**Good**	**Bad**	**Good**	**Good**	**Bad**	**Bad**

Three versions say Jesus could not be God because of His belief about God. That is heresy!

KJV	RVG	LBA	1865	1909	1960	NVI
23 Col. 1:17 ...and **by him** all things consist.	**por Él** ..... **by Him**	**en Él** ..... **in him**	**en él;** ..... **in him**	**por él** ..... **by him**	**en él** ..... **in him**	**por medio de él** ..... **through him**
Translation is... **Good**	**Good**	**Bad**	**Bad**	**Good**	**Bad**	**Bad**

Everything is held together "by" our Lord Jesus Christ. "In" Christ and "through" Christ are bad translations that make no sense.

	KJV	RVG	LBA	1865	1909	1960	NVI
24	Rev. 1:6 hath made us kings and priests unto God and his Father	para Dios y su Padre ..... unto God and his Father	para su Dios y Padre ..... unto his God and Father	para Dios y su Padre ..... unto God and his Father	para Dios y su Padre ..... unto God and his Father	para Dios, su Padre ..... unto God, his Father	de Dios su Padre ..... of God his Father
Translation is...	Good	Good	Bad	Good	Good	Bad	Bad

Correctly translated, this verse shows that Jesus is God. However, three versions strip away the deity of Christ. So instead of the word "God" correctly referring to Jesus, it refers to God the Father.

	KJV	RVG	LBA	1865	1909	1960	NVI
25	Luke 8:12 lest they should believe and **be saved.**	y sean salvos. ..... be saved.	y se salven. ..... be saved (save themselves).	no se salven creyendo. ..... are not saved (do not save themselves) believing.	y se salven. ..... be saved (**save themselves**).	y se salven. ..... be saved (save themselves).	y se salven. ..... be saved (save themselves).
Translation is...	Good	Good	Bad	Bad	Bad	Bad	Bad

The words "sean salvos," "los salvos," "serán salvos" have only one meaning: "be saved." But modern Bibles use "se salven," "se salvan," or "se salva," which can also mean "save themselves," an unscriptural doctrine. Same applies for following verse, Luke 13:23.

	KJV	RVG	LBA	1865	1909	1960	NVI
26	Luke 13:23 Lord, are there few that **be saved?**	serán salvos? ..... will be saved?	se salvan? ..... be saved (save themselves)?	se salvan? ..... be saved (save themselves)?	se salvan? ..... be saved (save themselves)?	se salvan? ..... be saved (save themselves)?	van a salvarse? ..... are going to be saved (save themselves)?
	Translation is...						
	Good	Good	Bad	Bad	Bad	Bad	Bad
27	1 Corinthians 1:18 but unto us which **are saved**	nosotros los salvos ..... us the saved	nosotros los salvos ..... us the saved	los que se salvan ..... that are saved, (save ourselves)	los que se salvan ..... that are saved, (save ourselves)	los que se salvan ..... that are saved, (save ourselves)	los que se salvan ..... that are saved (save ourselves)
	Translation is...						
	Good	Good	Good	Bad	Bad	Bad	Bad
28	2 Corinthians 2:15 in them that **are saved**	son salvos ..... are saved	se salvan ..... are saved, (save themselves)	son salvos ..... are saved	se salvan ..... are saved, (save themselves)	se salvan ..... are saved, (save themselves)	se salvan ..... are saved, (save themselves)
	Translation is...						
	Good	Good	Bad	Good	Bad	Bad	Bad

	KJV	RVG	LBA	1865	1909	1960	NVI
29	1 Thess. 2:16 that they might **be saved** *Translation is...*	sean salvos ..... be saved	se salven ..... be saved, (save themselves)	sean salvos ..... be saved	se salven ..... be saved, (save themselves)	se salven ..... be saved, (save themselves)	sean salvos ..... be saved
	Good	Good	Bad	Good	Bad	Bad	Good
30	1 Peter 4:18 And if the righteous scarcely **be saved** *Translation is...*	es salvo ..... be saved	se salva ..... be saved, (save themselves)	es dificultosa-mente salvo ..... is saved with difficulty	se salva ..... be saved; (save themselves)	se salva ..... be saved, (save themselves)	se salva ..... be saved, (save themselves)
	Good	Good	Bad	Good	Bad	Bad	Bad
31	Mark 9:24 **With tears** *Translation is...*	con lágrimas ..... with tears	These words deleted from this version.	con lágrimas ..... with tears	These words deleted from this version.	These words deleted from this version.	These words deleted from this version.
	Good	Good	Bad	Good	Bad	Bad	Bad

	KJV	RVG	LBA	1865	1909	1960	NVI
32	John 13:10 ye **are** clean, but not all.	vosotros **sois** limpios, aunque no todos. ..... and ye are (**permanently**) clean.	vosotros **estáis** limpios, pero no todos. ..... and ye **are** (**temporarily**) clean.	vosotros limpios **estáis**, aunque no todos. ..... and ye **are** (**temporarily**) clean.	vosotros limpios **estáis**, aunque no todos. ..... and ye **are** (**temporarily**) clean.	vosotros limpios **estáis**, aunque no todos. ..... and ye **are** (**temporarily**) clean.	ustedes ya **están** limpios, aunque no todos. ..... And ye **are** (**temporarily**) already clean.
Translation is...	**Good**	**Good**	**Bad**	**Bad**	**Bad**	**Bad**	**Bad**

Two different Spanish words can be translated "are." One describes a temporary condition. The other is permanent. The RVG is the only Spanish Bible that uses the correct Spanish word, teaching that salvation is eternal, and not something that only lasts for a short while.

	KJV	RVG	LBA	1865	1909	1960	NVI
33	John 13:11 For he knew who should betray him; therefore said he, Ye **are** not all clean.	No **sois** limpios todos. ..... Ye **are** (**permanently**) not all clean.	No todos **estáis** limpios. ..... Ye **are** (**temporarily**) not all clean.	No **estáis** limpios todos. ..... Ye **are** (**temporarily**) not all clean.	No **estáis** limpios todos. ..... Ye **are** (**temporarily**) not all clean.	No **estáis** limpios todos. ..... Ye **are** (**temporarily**) not all clean.	no todos **estaban** limpios. ..... not all **were** (**past tense**) clean.
Translation is...	**Good**	**Good**	**Bad**	**Bad**	**Bad**	**Bad**	**Bad**

	KJV	RVG	LBA	1865	1909	1960	NVI
34	John 15:3 Now ye are clean through the word which I have spoken unto you.	vosotros **sois** limpios ..... **ye are (permanently)** clean	Vosotros ... **estáis limpios** ..... ye are **(temporarily)** clean	vosotros **sois** limpios ..... **ye are (permanently)** clean	vosotros **sois** limpios ..... **ye are (permanently)** clean	vosotros **estáis** limpios ..... ye are **(temporarily)** clean	Ustedes ya **están limpios** ..... Ye already are **(temporarily)** clean
Translation is...	Good	Good	Bad	Good	Good	Bad	Bad
35	Psalm 104:4 his ministers **a flaming fire:**	sus ministros **fuego flameante.** ..... his ministers a **flaming fire.**	**las llamas de fuego** sus ministros. ..... **the flames of fire** his ministers.	sus ministros **al fuego flameante.** ..... his ministers **to the flaming fire.**	sus ministros **al fuego flameante.** ..... his ministers **to the flaming fire.**	y a **las flamas de fuego** sus ministros. ..... and to the **flames of fire** his ministers.	**las llamas de fuego** tus servidores. ..... **the flames of fire** his servants.
Translation is...	Good	Good	Bad	Bad	Bad	Bad	Bad

The KJV and the RVG say that God makes his ministers "a flaming fire." But the 1865, 1909 and 1960 say his ministers are going "to the flaming fire." Sounds like His servants are going to hell. The LBA and NVI speak about fire, not men, being His servants.

KJV	RVG	LBA	1865	1909	1960	NVI
36 Galatians 5:4 Christ is **become of no effect** unto you, whosoever of you are justified by the law;	Cristo ha venido **a ser sin efecto** para vosotros ..... Christ has come **to be without effect unto you**	De Cristo **os habéis separado** ..... From Christ ye have **separated**	Cristo se ha hecho para **vosotros inútil,** ..... Christ has been **made unto you useless**	**Vacíos sois de Cristo** ..... **Ye are empty of Christ**	De Cristo os **desligasteis** ..... From Christ ye **have been un-tied, unraveled or freed**	**han roto con Cristo** ..... **have been broken with Christ**
Translation is... Good	Good	Bad	Good	Good	Bad	Bad
37 1 Corinthians 9:27 I myself should be **a castaway.**	yo mismo venga **a ser reprobado.** ..... come to be a **reprobate.**	yo mismo sea **descalificado.** ..... come to be **disqualified.**	no sea yo mismo **reprobado.** ..... do not come to be a **reprobate.**	yo mismo venga **á ser reprobado.** ..... come to be a **reprobate.**	yo mismo venga **a ser eliminado.** ..... come to be **eliminated.**	yo mismo quede **descalificado.** ..... should be **disqualified.**
Translation is... Good	Good	Good	Good	Good	Bad	Good

This verse has nothing to do with losing your salvation. The KJV uses the word "castaway," meaning "to be put to the side and not used anymore (useless)." Most Spanish Bibles use the word "reprobate," which means "having failed the test" or "useless." These agree with the Greek word. But the 1960 means that God takes away the salvation, or the life of the saved person.

38	KJV	RVG	LBA	1865	1909	1960	NVI
Hebrews 2:16 For verily he **took** not on *him the nature of* angels; but he **took** on *him* the seed of Abraham.		no **tomó** *para sí la naturaleza de* los ángeles, sino que **tomó** la de la simiente de Abraham. ····· he **took** not *on him the nature of* the angels, but he **took** the nature of the seed of Abraham.	no **ayuda** a los ángeles, sino que **ayuda** a la descendencia de Abraham. ····· he does not **help** the angels, but he **helps** the descendents of Abraham.	no **toma** a los ángeles, mas **toma** a la simiente de Abraham. ····· he **takes** not the angels, but he **takes** the seed of Abraham.	no **tomó** á los ángeles, sino á la simiente de Abraham **tomó**. ····· he **took** not the angels, but the seed of Abraham he **took**.	no **socorrió** a los ángeles, sino que **socorrió** a la descendencia de Abraham. ····· he did not **help** the angels, but he **helped** the descendents of Abraham.	no vino **en auxilio de** los ángeles sino de los descendientes de Abraham. ····· he did not come **to the aid of** angels, but the descendents of Abraham.
Translation is....	Good	Good	Bad	Good	Good	Bad	Bad

The RVG is clear and correct. Jesus put on human flesh. He took on Him the seed of Abraham. But the 1960, LBA and NVI say He "did not help the angels" but He "helped the descendents of Abraham." The Greek words do not mean helping. Jesus took on Him human flesh to save us. He never sinned and for that reason He could and did pay for our sins as God in human flesh.

	KJV	RVG	LBA	1865	1909	1960	NVI
39	1 Peter 1:5 Who are kept by the power of God through faith **unto** salvation...	para la salvación ..... unto salvation	para la salvación ..... unto salvation	para alcanzar la salvación ..... to reach salvation	para alcanzar la salud ..... to reach health (spiritual health salvation)	para alcanzar la salvación ..... to reach salvation	hasta que llegue la salvación ..... until salvation arrives
	Translation is...						
	Good	Good	Good	Bad	Bad	Bad	Good

The correct translation is "unto salvation." "To reach or obtain" does not appear in the Greek, and teaches a false doctrine.

	KJV	RVG	LBA	1865	1909	1960	NVI
40	1 Peter 2:2 As newborn babes, desire the sincere milk of the word, that ye may grow thereby:	para que por ella crezcáis ..... that ye may grow by it;	para que por ella crezcáis para salvación ..... that ye may grow unto (or to have) salvation	para que por ella crezcáis ..... that ye may grow by it:	para que por ella crezcáis en salud ..... that ye may grow by it in salvation:	para que por ella crezcáis para salvación ..... that ye may grow unto (or to have) salvation	por medio de ella, crecerán en su salvación ..... So, through it, ye may grow up in your salvation
	Translation is...						
	Good	Good	Bad	Good	Good	Bad	Good

This is about Christians growing spiritually, but the LBA and 1960 say we must grow in order to obtain salvation. More false doctrine.

	KJV	RVG	LBA	1865	1909	1960	NVI
41	1 Peter 3:21 **The like figure** whereunto even baptism doth also now save us	**A la figura** de lo cual el bautismo que ahora corresponde nos salva • • • • • **The like figure** whereunto baptism that now corresponds saves us	Y correspondiendo a esto, el bautismo ahora os salva • • • • • And corresponding to that, baptism now saves you	**A la figura** de la cual el bautismo, que ahora corresponde, nos salva a nosotros también, • • • • • **The like figure** whereunto baptism that now corresponds saves us also	**A la figura** de la cual el bautismo que ahora corresponde nos salva • • • • • **The like figure** whereunto baptism that now corresponds saves us	El bautismo que corresponde a esto ahora nos salva • • • • • The baptism that corresponds to this now saves us	la cual simboliza el bautismo que ahora los salva también a ustedes. • • • • • which symbolizes baptism that now saves you also.
Translation is...	**Good**	**Good**	**Bad**	**Good**	**Good**	**Bad**	**Bad**

Baptism is a figure that represents the death, burial and resurrection of our Saviour. It does not save us from hell or clean up our sins. It is merely "a figure." By removing the words "the like figure," which appear in the Greek text, the LBA, 1960 and NVI teach a completely false doctrine that baptism saves us. There is no reason to take out the Greek word, unless you believe that baptism saves.

216 GOD'S BIBLE IN SPANISH

KJV	RVG	LBA	1865	1909	1960	NVI
42						
Deuteronomy 32:22 and shall burn unto the lowest **hell,**	lo profundo del **infierno** ..... the lowest **hell**	las **profundidades del Seol** ..... the lowest of **Sheol**	hasta el **profundo** ..... unto the **deep**	hasta el **profundo** ..... unto the **deep**	hasta las **profundidades del Seol** ..... unto the lowest of **Sheol**	hasta **lo profundo del abismo** ..... to the depth of the abyss
Translation is...						
Good	**Good**	**Bad**	**Bad**	**Bad**	**Bad**	**Bad**

The following several verses talk about hell, a very real place. But many translators treat it as mythology, or they personally don't believe it exists so they give it other names to confuse or mislead the reader. But both the Hebrew and Greek words refer to that horrible place, hell. It is dishonest and misleading to translate these words any other way. "Sheol" is just a transliteration of the Hebrew word for hell. Why translate all other words but not this one?

KJV	RVG	LBA	1865	1909	1960	NVI
43						
2 Samuel 22:6 The sorrows of **hell** compassed me about;	los dolores del **infierno** ..... The pains of **hell**	los lazos del **Seol** ..... The ties of **Sheol**	las cuerdas del **sepulcro** ..... the cords of the **sepulcher**	los dolores del **infierno** ..... The pains of **hell**	Ligaduras del **Seol** ..... The cords of **Sheol**	los lazos del **sepulcro** ..... The ties of the **sepulcher**
Translation is...						
Good	**Good**	**Bad**	**Bad**	**Good**	**Bad**	**Bad**

A sepulcher is "a grave, a tomb or a burial place," not even close to the Greek word used.

	KJV	RVG	LBA	1865	1909	1960	NVI
44	Ps. 86:13 thou hast delivered my soul from the lowest **hell**.	del más profundo **infierno** ..... the lowest **hell**	de las profundidades del **Seol** ..... depths of **Sheol**	del **hoyo** profundo ..... the lowest **pit**	del **hoyo** profundo ..... the lowest **pit**	de las profundidades del **Seol** ..... depths of **Sheol**	de caer en el **sepulcro** ..... into the **sepulcher**
Translation is...	**Good**	**Good**	**Bad**	**Bad**	**Bad**	**Bad**	**Bad**

One can dig a pit out in his back yard. That is not what this verse is talking about.

	KJV	RVG	LBA	1865	1909	1960	NVI
45	Prov 9:18 *and that* her guests *are* in the depths of **hell**.	lo profundo del **infierno** ..... the depths of **hell**	las profundidades del **Seol** ..... the depths of **Sheol**	los profundos de la **sepultura** ..... the depths of the **grave**	los profundos de la **sepultura** ..... the depths of the **grave**	lo profundo del **Seol** ..... the depths of **Sheol**	al fondo de la **fosa** ..... the bottom of the **pit**
Translation is...	**Good**	**Good**	**Bad**	**Bad**	**Bad**	**Bad**	**Bad**

Using the word "grave" instead of the correct translation "hell" is yet another attempt to mislead and confuse readers.

	KJV	RVG	LBA	1865	1909	1960	NVI
46	Proverbs 27:20 Hell and destruction are never full;	El infierno y la perdición ..... Hell and perdition	El Seol y el Abadón ..... Sheol and Abaddon	El sepulcro y la perdición ..... The sepulcher and perdition	El sepulcro y la perdición ..... The sepulcher and perdition	El Seol y el Abadón ..... Sheol and Abaddon	El sepulcro, la muerte ..... The sepulcher, death
Translation is...	Good	Good	Bad	Bad	Bad	Bad	Bad
47	Habakkuk 2:5 who enlargeth his desire as hell	ensancha como el infierno ..... enlargeth as hell	ensancha su garganta como el Seol ..... enlarges his throat as Sheol	ensanchó como un osario ..... enlarged as an ossuary	ensanchó como el infierno ..... enlarged as hell	ensanchó como el Seol ..... enlarged like Sheol	como el sepulcro ..... as the sepulcher
Translation is...	Good	Good	Bad	Bad	Good	Bad	Bad

An ossuary is a place to keep dead men's bones. A completely wrong translation.

48

KJV	RVG	LBA	1865	1909	1960	NVI
Matthew 11:23 shalt be brought down to **hell**:	hasta el **infierno** ..... down to **hell**	¡Hasta el **Hades** descenderás! ..... Unto **Hades** shalt thou descend	hasta los **infiernos** ..... down to the **hells**	hasta los **infiernos** ..... down to the **hells**	hasta el **Hades** ..... down to **Hades**	hasta el **abismo** ..... unto the **abyss**

Translation is...

KJV	RVG	LBA	1865	1909	1960	NVI
Good	Good	Bad	Bad	Bad	Bad	Bad

"Hells" is a bad translation because there is only one hell.

49

KJV	RVG	LBA	1865	1909	1960	NVI
Matthew 16:18 and the gates of **hell** shall not prevail against it.	las puertas del **infierno** ..... gates of **hell**	las puertas del **Hades** ..... gates of **Hades**	las puertas del **infierno** ..... gates of **hell**	las puertas del **infierno** ..... gates of **hell**	las puertas del **Hades** ..... gates of **Hades**	las puertas del **reino de la muerte** ..... gates of the **kingdom of death**

Translation is...

KJV	RVG	LBA	1865	1909	1960	NVI
Good	Good	Bad	Good	Good	Bad	Bad

	KJV	RVG	LBA	1865	1909	1960	NVI
50 Mark 9:43	than having two hands to go into **hell**	ir al **infierno** ..... go to **hell**	ir a la **infierno** ..... go to **hell**	ir al **infierno** ..... go to **hell**	ir á la **Gehenna** ..... go to **Gehenna**	ir al **infierno** ..... go to **hell**	ir con las dos manos al **infierno** ..... go with both hands to **hell**
Translation is...	Good	Good	Good	Good	Bad	Good	Good

"Gehenna" is another Greek word that translators chose not to translate, once again hiding the meaning of the word "hell."

	KJV	RVG	LBA	1865	1909	1960	NVI
51 Mark 9:47 to be cast into **hell fire:**		echado al **fuego del infierno:** ..... cast to the **fire of hell**	echado al **infierno;** ..... cast into **hell,** (omitted the word "**fire**")	echado al **fuego del infierno:** ..... cast to the **fire of hell**	echado á la **Gehenna;** ..... cast to **Gehenna**	echado al **infierno,** ..... cast to **hell,** (omitted the word "**fire**")	arrojado... al **infierno,** ..... thrown ... into **hell,** (omitted the word "**fire**")
Translation is...	Good	Good	Good but weak	Good	Bad	Good but weak	Good but weak

The correct translation is "hell fire" or "fire of hell." Without the word "fire" it is much weaker.

	KJV	RVG	LBA	1865	1909	1960	NVI
52	Luke 10:15 shalt be thrust down to **hell**.	hasta el **infierno** ..... down to **hell**	Hasta el **Hades** ..... To **Hades**	hasta **los infiernos** ..... down to **the hells**	hasta **los infiernos** ..... down to **the hells**	hasta el **Hades** ..... down to **Hades**	hasta el **abismo.** ..... unto the **abyss**
	Translation is...						
	Good	**Good**	**Bad**	**Bad**	**Bad**	**Bad**	**Bad**

For more badly translated verses on hell, see Job 11:8, Psalm 9:17; 16:10; 18:5; 55:15; 139:8; 116:3; 5:5, Prov. 7:27; 15:11; 15:24; 23:14, Isaiah 5:14; 14:15; 14:9; 28:15; 28:18; 57:9, Ezekiel 31:16; 31:17; 32:21; 32:27, Amos 9:2, Jonah 2:2, Mark 9:45, Luke 12:5; 16:23, Acts 2:27; 2:31, Revelation 1:18; 6:8; 20:13; 20:14.

	KJV	RVG	LBA	1865	1909	1960	NVI
53	Mark 9:24 **Lord**, I believe; help thou mine unbelief.	**Señor**, creo, ayuda mi incredulidad. ..... **Lord**, I believe, help my unbelief.	Creo; *ayudame en mi* incredulidad. ..... I believe; help *me in* my unbelief.	Creo, **Señor**: ayuda mi incredulidad. ..... I believe, **Lord**: help my unbelief.	Creo, ayuda mi incredulidad. ..... I believe, help my unbelief.	Creo, ayuda mi incredulidad. ..... I believe, help my unbelief.	¡Sí creo! ... ¡Ayúdame en mi poca fe! ..... Yes I believe! ... help me in my little faith!
	Translation is...						
	Good	**Good**	**Bad**	**Good**	**Bad**	**Bad**	**Bad**

The word "Lord" is removed, taking away the fact that Jesus is Lord.

	KJV	RVG	LBA	1865	1909	1960	NVI
54	Mark 11:10 in the name of the Lord	en el nombre del Señor ..... in the name of the Lord	These words are missing from this version.	en el nombre del Señor ..... in the name of the Lord	These words are missing from this version.	These words are missing from this version.	These words are missing from this version.
Translation is...	Good	Good	Bad	Good	Bad	Bad	Bad

The words "in the name of the Lord" are missing, even though they appear in the Greek text.

	KJV	RVG	LBA	1865	1909	1960	NVI
55	Luke 23:42 he said unto Jesus, Lord, remember me	Jesús: Señor, acuérdate de mí ..... Jesús: Lord, remember me	Jesús, acuér-date de mí ..... Jesús, remember me	Jesús: Señor, acuérdate de mí ..... Jesús: Lord, remember me	Jesús: Acuér-date de mí ..... Jesús: Remember me	Jesús: Acuér-date de mí ..... Jesús: Remember me	Jesús, acuér-date de mí ..... Jesús, remember me
Translation is...	Good	Good	Bad	Good	Bad	Bad	Bad

The word "Lord" is missing, removing the fact that Jesus is Lord.

SPANISH BIBLE VERSE COMPARISONS 223

	KJV	RVG	LBA	1865	1909	1960	NVI
56	Luke 4:41 Thou art **Christ** the Son of God.	Tú eres **Cristo**, el Hijo de Dios. ..... Thou art **Christ**, the Son of God.	¡Tú eres el Hijo de Dios! ..... Thou art the Son of God!	Tú eres el **Cristo**, el Hijo de Dios; ..... Thou art the **Christ**, the Son of God;	Tú eres el Hijo de Dios. ..... Thou art the Son of God.	Tú eres el Hijo de Dios. ..... Thou art the Son of God.	¡Tú eres el Hijo de Dios! ..... You are the Son of God!
Translation is...	Good	Good	Bad	Good	Bad	Bad	Bad

The word "Christ" is removed, hiding the fact that Jesus is the Christ.

	KJV	RVG	LBA	1865	1909	1960	NVI
57	Acts 3:26 God, having raised up his **Son Jesus**	su **Hijo Jesús** ..... his **Son Jesus**	su **Siervo** ..... his **Servant**	su **Hijo Jesús** ..... his **Son Jesus**	su **Hijo** ..... his **Son**	su **Hijo** ..... his **Son**	su **siervo** ..... his **servant**
Translation is...	Good	Good	Bad	Good	Bad	Bad	Bad

Is Jesus God's "Son" or His "servant?" Huge difference. "Jesus" is missing from the 1909 and 1960. The LBA and NVI change "son" to "servant".

	KJV	RVG	LBA	1865	1909	1960	NVI
58	Acts 9:29 And he spake boldly in the name of the Lord **Jesus**,	en el nombre del Señor **Jesús** ..... in the name of the Lord **Jesus**	También hablaba ..... He also spake	en el nombre del Señor **Jesús** ..... in the name of the Lord Jesus	en el nombre del Señor ..... in the name of the Lord	en el nombre del Señor ..... in the name of the Lord	Conversaba ..... He conversed
Translation is...	**Good**	**Good**	**Bad**	**Good**	**Bad**	**Bad**	**Bad**
59	Acts 7:30 there appeared to him in the wilderness of mount Sina an angel **of the Lord**	el Ángel **del Señor** le apareció ..... the Angel **of the Lord** appeared to him	le apareció un ángel ..... an angel appeared to him	el ángel **del Señor** le apareció ..... the angel of the Lord appeared to him	un ángel le apareció ..... an angel appeared to him	un ángel se le apareció ..... an angel appeared to him	se le apareció un ángel ..... an angel appeared to him
Translation is...	**Good**	**Good**	**Bad**	**Good**	**Bad**	**Bad**	**Bad**

The words "of the Lord" were removed from the LBA, 1909, 1960, and NVI.

	KJV	RVG	LBA	1865	1909	1960	NVI
60	Acts 22:16 wash away thy sins, calling on the name **of the Lord.**	invocando el nombre **del Señor.** ..... calling on the name **of the Lord.**	invocando **su nombre.** ..... calling on **his** name.	invocando el nombre **del Señor.** ..... calling on the name **of the Lord.**	invocando **su nombre.** ..... calling on **his** name.	invocando **su nombre.** ..... calling on **his** name.	invocando **su nombre.** ..... calling on **his** name.
Translation is...	Good	Good	Bad	Good	Bad	Bad	Bad

The words "of the Lord" are replaced with "his," hiding the fact that the Lord washes away sins.

	KJV	RVG	LBA	1865	1909	1960	NVI
61	Acts 8:16 were baptized in the name of the **Lord** Jesus.	en el nombre del **Señor** Jesús. ..... in the name of the **Lord** Jesus.	en el nombre del **Señor** Jesús. ..... in the name of the **Lord** Jesus.	en el nombre del **Señor** Jesús. ..... in the name of the **Lord** Jesus.	en el nombre de Jesús. ..... in the name of Jesus.	en el nombre de Jesús. ..... in the name of Jesus.	en el nombre del **Señor** Jesús. ..... in the name of the **Lord** Jesus.
Translation is...	Good	Good	Good	Good	Bad	Bad	Good

KJV	RVG	LBA	1865	1909	1960	NVI
62 Acts 15:11 through the grace of the Lord Jesus **Christ** we shall be saved	gracia del Señor **Jesucristo** ····· grace of the Lord Jesus **Christ**	gracia del Señor Jesús ····· grace of the Lord Jesus	gracia del Señor Jesu **Cristo** ····· grace of the Lord Jesus **Christ**	gracia del Señor Jesús ····· grace of the Lord Jesus	gracia del Señor Jesús ····· grace of the Lord Jesus	gracia de nuestro Señor Jesús ····· grace of our Lord Jesus
Translation is... **Good**	**Good**	**Bad**	**Good**	**Bad**	**Bad**	**Bad**
63 Romans 1:3 Concerning his Son **Jesus Christ our Lord**	su Hijo **Jesucristo, nuestro Señor** ····· his Son **Jesus Christ, our Lord**	su Hijo ····· Concerning his Son	su Hijo **Jesu Cristo, Señor nuestro** ····· his Son **Jesus Christ, our Lord**	su Hijo ····· Concerning his Son	su Hijo, **nuestro Señor Jesucristo,** ····· his Son, **our Lord Jesus Christ**	su Hijo ····· his Son
Translation is... **Good**	**Good**	**Bad**	**Good**	**Bad**	**Good**	**Bad**

The LBA, 1909, and NVI left out the words "Jesus Christ our Lord," even though they appear in the Greek. For more examples of the name of the Lord Jesus Christ being changed, see 1 Corinthians 9:1; 4:10; 5:18.

64

	KJV	RVG	LBA	1865	1909	1960	NVI
Romans 1:16	For I am not ashamed of the gospel **of Christ**	del evangelio **de Cristo** ..... the gospel **of Christ**	del evangelio ..... the gospel	del evangelio **de Cristo** ..... the gospel **of Christ**	del evangelio ..... the gospel	del evangelio ..... the gospel	del evangelio ..... the gospel
Translation is...	Good	Good	Bad	Good	Bad	Bad	Bad

The words "of Christ" are left out, although they appear in the Greek text.

65

	KJV	RVG	LBA	1865	1909	1960	NVI
Ephesians 3:9	who created all things by **Jesus Christ:**	creó todas las cosas **por Jesucristo** ..... created all things **by Jesus Christ**	creador de todas las cosas ..... creator of all things	creó todas las cosas **por Jesu Cristo** ..... created all things **by Jesus Christ**	crió todas las cosas ..... created all things	creó todas las cosas ..... created all things	creador de todas las cosas ..... creator of all things
Translation is...	Good	Good	Bad	Good	Bad	Bad	Bad

The LBA, 1909, 1960, and NVI took out "Jesus Christ," although it appears in the Greek text.

228 GOD'S BIBLE IN SPANISH

	KJV	RVG	LBA	1865	1909	1960	NVI
66 2 Thessalonians 2:2	the day of **Christ** is **at hand.**	el día de **Cristo** está **cerca.** ..... the day of **Christ** is **close.**	el día del **Señor** ha **llegado.** ..... the day of the **Lord has come.**	el día de **Cristo** esté **cerca.** ..... the day of **Christ** is **close.**	el día del **Señor** esté **cerca.** ..... the day of the **Lord** is **close.**	el día del **Señor** está **cerca.** ..... the day of the **Lord** is **close.**	¡Ya llegó el día del **Señor!** ..... The day of the **Lord has come!**
Translation is...	Good	Good	Bad	Good	Bad	Bad	Bad

There is a big difference between the day of Christ being "close" or "at hand" (meaning it is in the future), and "has come" (has already happened)! The Greek says "Christ," not "Lord."

	KJV	RVG	LBA	1865	1909	1960	NVI
67 Matthew 15:8	**draweth nigh unto me with their mouth,**	**se acerca a mí con su boca,** ..... **draweth nigh unto me with their mouth,**	These words were deleted from this version.	**con su boca se acerca a mí,** ..... **with their mouth draweth nigh unto me,**	These words were deleted from this version.	These words were deleted from this version.	These words were deleted from this version.
Translation is...	Good	Good	Bad	Good	Bad	Bad	Bad

	KJV	RVG	LBA	1865	1909	1960	NVI
68	Luke 2:40 and waxed strong **in spirit**	se fortalecía **en espíritu** ····· waxed strong **in spirit**	se fortalecía ····· waxed strong	era confortado **en espíritu** ····· was strength-ened **in spirit**	fortalecíase ····· waxed strong	se fortalecía ····· waxed strong	se fortalecía ····· waxed strong
Translation is...	Good	Good	Bad	Good	Bad	Bad	Bad

The words "in spirit" are missing in the LBA, 1909, 1960 and NVI.

	KJV	RVG	LBA	1865	1909	1960	NVI
69	Acts 2:41 Then they that **gladly** received his word	que **con gozo** recibieron su palabra ····· that **with joy** received his word	que habían recibido su palabra ····· that had received his word	que recibieron **con gusto** su palabra ····· that received **with pleasure** his word	que recibieron su palabra ····· that received his word	que recibieron su palabra ····· that received his word	que recibieron su mensaje ····· that received his message
Translation is...	Good	Good	Bad	Good	Bad	Bad	Bad

Although they appear in the Greek text, the words "with joy" or "gladly" are missing in four versions.

	KJV	RVG	LBA	1865	1909	1960	NVI
70 Acts 15:17-18 Known unto God are all his works from the beginning of the world.		desde la eternidad ..... from the eternity	desde tiempos antiguos ..... since ancient times	desde la eternidad ..... from the eternity	desde el siglo ..... from forever	desde tiempos antiguos ..... from old times	desde tiempos antiguos ..... from ancient times
Translation is...		Good	Bad	Good	Good	Bad	Bad

The original text says that God is eternal and has always known everything. But the LBA, 1960 and NVI changed it to teach the false doctrine that either God came into existence in ancient times or His knowledge started in ancient times.

	KJV	RVG	LBA	1865	1909	1960	NVI
71 1 Corinthians 7:5 give yourselves to **fasting and prayer;**		ayuno y oración ..... fasting and prayer	la oración ..... prayer	ayuno y en oración ..... fasting and prayer	la oración ..... prayer	la oración ..... calmly in prayer	la oración ..... prayer
Translation is...		Good	Bad	Good	Bad	Bad	Bad

Although the word "fasting" appears in the Greek, it is removed. The 1960 added "calmly" even though it is not in the Greek.

	KJV	RVG	LBA	1865	1909	1960	NVI
72	Leviticus 2:12 they shall not be **burnt** on the altar for a sweet savour.	quemarán ····· be burnt	ascenderán ····· ascend	subirán ····· rise	subirán ····· rise	subirán ····· rise	pondrán ····· put
Translation is...	**Good**	**Good**	**Bad**	**Bad**	**Bad**	**Bad**	**Bad**

This offering was not to be burnt so the smell of the burning would not rise. The word "rise" does not explain the point very well. "Put" (NVI) explains even less.

	KJV	RVG	LBA	1865	1909	1960	NVI
73	Leviticus 16:8, 10, 26 **scapegoat**	el macho cabrío de escapatoria ····· scapegoat	el macho cabrío expiatorio ····· scapegoat	Azazel ····· Untranslated Hebrew word	Azazel ····· Untranslated Hebrew word	Azazel ····· Untranslated Hebrew word	el macho cabrío (que soltará en el desierto) ····· male goat (that will be released in the desert)
Translation is...	**Good**	**Good**	**Good**	**Bad**	**Bad**	**Bad**	**Good**

"Scapegoat" conveys exactly what the Hebrew word means. But the untranslated Hebrew word cannot be understood.

232 GOD'S BIBLE IN SPANISH

	KJV	RVG	LBA	1865	1909	1960	NVI
74	Judges 3:7 and **forgat** the LORD their God	**olvidaron a** Jehová su Dios ..... **forgat** Jehovah their God	**olvidaron al** SEÑOR su Dios ..... **forgat** the LORD their God	**olvidados de** Jehová su Dios ..... **forgotten of** Jehovah their God	**olvidados de** Jehová su Dios ..... **forgotten of** Jehovah their God	**olvidaron a** Jehová su Dios ..... **forgat** Jehovah their God	se olvidaron del SEÑOR su Dios ..... **they forgat** the LORD their God
Translation is...	Good	Good	Good	Bad	Bad	Good	Good

Defective Bibles change the verse from saying that "they forgot their God" to the opposite, that "God forgot them."

	KJV	RVG	LBA	1865	1909	1960	NVI
75	Judges 20:43 *and* chased them, *and* trode them down **with ease** over against Gibeah	los persiguieron y **fácilmente** los aplastaron ..... chased them and **easily flattened** them	lo persiguieron **sin tregua** y lo aplastaron ..... pursued him **relentlessly** and flattened him	los siguieron, y hollaron desde **Menual,** ..... followed and trampled them from **Menual,**	los acosaron y hollaron, desde **Menuchâ** ..... pursued and trampled them, from **Menucha**	los acosaron y hollaron desde **Menuha** ..... pursued and trampled them from **Menuha**	los persiguieron y los aplastaron **con facilidad** ..... pursued them and flattened them **with ease**
Translation is...	Good	Good	Bad	Bad	Bad	Bad	Good

mᵉnûchâh, (Menucha) Strong's #4496 is a Hebrew word not translated in the 1865, 1909 and 1960. Menucha is not a place. The word refers to how easily they won the battle. "Relentlessly" (LBA) is also incorrect. The LBA also changes "them" to "him."

76

KJV	RVG	LBA	1865	1909	1960	NVI
2 Samuel 14:14 neither doth God **respect** *any* person:	Dios no **hace acepción** de personas ..... God does not **respect** persons	Dios no **quita** la vida ..... God **does** not **take** life	ni Dios le **quitará** la vida ..... neither **will** God **take** his life	ni Dios **quita** la vida ..... neither **does** God **take** life	ni Dios **quita** la vida ..... neither **does** God **take** life	Dios no nos **arrebata** la vida ..... God does not **take away** our life
Translation is...						
Good	Good	Bad	Bad	Bad	Bad	Bad

God does take life away from many but He never respects persons. He is always fair and just. The word "take" incorrectly translated.

77

KJV	RVG	LBA	1865	1909	1960	NVI
2 Samuel 21:19 Elhanan...slew *the brother of* Goliath	**mató al hermano de** Goliat ..... **slew the brother of** Goliath	Omits the words, **"the brother of (al hermano de)"**	**hirió al hermano de** Goliat ..... slew **the brother** of Goliath	Omits the words, **"the brother of"**	Omits the words, **"the brother of"**	Omits the words, **"the brother of"**
Translation is...						
Good	Good	Bad	Good	Bad	Bad	Bad

Without the words "the brother of," the text falsely says that Elhanan killed Goliath. 1 Chronicles 20:5 includes the words "the brother of."

KJV	RVG	LBA	1865	1909	1960	NVI
78						
2 Kings 2:9 let a **double portion of thy spirit** be upon me.	una **doble por-ción de tu espíritu** sea sobre mí. ····· **a double por-tion of thy spirit** be upon me.	**las dos partes** de tu espíritu sean sobre mí. ····· **the two parts** of thy spirit be upon me.	**las dos partes** de tu espíritu sean sobre mí. ····· **the two parts** of thy spirit be upon me.	**las dos partes** de tu espíritu sean sobre mí. ····· **the two parts** of thy spirit be upon me.	una **doble por-ción de tu espíritu** sea sobre mí. ····· **a double por-tion of thy spirit** be upon me.	el heredero de tu espíritu **por partida doble** ····· the heir of thy spirit **by a double part**
Translation is...						
Good	**Good**	**Bad**	**Bad**	**Bad**	**Good**	**Bad**

The words "double portion" make perfect sense. The words "the two parts of thy spirit" makes no sense at all.

KJV	RVG	LBA	1865	1909	1960	NVI
79						
Psalm 68:11 great *was* the company of **those that published *it*.**	el ejército de aquellos que **la publicaban** ····· the army of **those that published it.**	**las mujeres que anuncian las buenas nuevas** ····· the **women that announce the good tidings**	**de las evangelizantes** ····· of the **women evangelists**	De las **evangelizantes** ····· Of the **women evangelists**	las que llevaban **buenas nuevas** ····· **women that brought good tidings.**	de **mensajeras** la proclaman ····· of **female messengers** proclaim it:
Translation is...						
Good	**Good**	**Bad**	**Bad**	**Bad**	**Bad**	**Bad**

This is not only a bad translation, but it violates God's command against women preachers.

	KJV	RVG	LBA	1865	1909	1960	NVI
80							
	Ecclesiastes 3:15 God **requireth** that which is past.	Dios **demanda** lo que pasó ..... God **demands** that which is past.	Dios **busca** lo que pasó. ..... God **seeks** that which is past.	Dios **restaura** lo que pasó. ..... God **restores** that which is past.	Dios **restaura** lo que pasó. ..... God **restores** that which is past.	Dios **restaura** lo que pasó. ..... God **restores** that which is past.	Dios **hace que** la historia **se repita.** ..... God **makes** the story re-**peat itself.**
	Translation is...						
	Good	**Good**	**Good but weak**	**Bad**	**Bad**	**Bad**	**Bad**

The Greek text says "demands" or "requires." Modern translators simply changed it to "restores," which is completely wrong.

	KJV	RVG	LBA	1865	1909	1960	NVI
81							
	Ezekiel 26:18 shall be troubled at thy **departure.**	se espantarán de tu **partida.** ..... shall be frightened at thy **departure.**	se espantan de tu **fin.** ..... are frightened at thy **end.**	y espantarse han de tu **salida** ..... shall be frightened at thy **departure**	se espantarán de tu **éxito.** ..... shall be frightened at thy **success.**	se espantarán a causa de tu **fin.** ..... shall be fright-ened because of thy **end.**	se aterrorizan ante tu **debacle** ..... are terrified before your **debacle.**
	Translation is...						
	Good	**Good**	**Good**	**Good**	**Bad**	**Good**	**Bad**

The Hebrew word אֵצֵא (yatsa') refers to a departure, or an end, not a success or debacle. *Éxito* rarely means "end."

	KJV	RVG	LBA	1865	1909	1960	NVI
82	Hosea 3:3 thou shalt not be for *another* man: so will I also be for thee.	lo mismo *haré* yo por ti. ..... the same I *will do* for thee.	yo también seré para ti. ..... I also will be for thee.	ni tampoco yo vendré á ti. ..... neither *will* I *come* to thee.	ni tampoco yo vendré á ti. ..... neither *will* I *come* to thee.	lo mismo haré yo contigo. ..... the same will I do with thee.	¡Ni yo te voy a tocar! ..... Neither am I going to touch you!
Translation is...	Good	Good	Good	Bad	Bad	Good	Bad

The 1865, 1909 and NVI state that after Hosea bought back his wife he would NOT be with her. But the correct translation is that he WOULD be with her. This is especially important because, as with Hosea's wife, God received his people back even after they ran around in spiritual adultery.

	KJV	RVG	LBA	1865	1909	1960	NVI
83	Matthew 2:1, 7, 16 wise men	sabios ..... wise men	magos ..... magicians or sorcerers	magos ..... magicians or sorcerers	magos ..... magicians or sorcerers	magos ..... magicians or sorcerers	sabios ..... wise men
Translation is...	Good	Good	Bad	Bad	Bad	Bad	Good

Another horrible translation. The Greek says "wise men." Yet many modern Bible translators used the words "magicians or sorcerers." Completely wrong.

	KJV	RVG	LBA	1865	1909	1960	NVI
84	**Mark 1:2** As it is written in **the prophets**	Como está escrito en **los profetas** • • • • • As it is written in **the prophets**	Como está escrito en **el profeta Isaías** • • • • • As it is written in **the prophet Isaiah**	Como está escrito en **los profetas** • • • • • As it is written in **the prophets**	Como está escrito en **Isaías el profeta** • • • • • As it is written in Isaiah the prophet	Como está escrito en **Isaías el profeta** • • • • • As it is written in **Isaiah the prophet**	como está escrito en **el profeta Isaías** • • • • • As it is written in **Isaiah the prophet**
	Translation is... **Good**	**Good**	**Bad**	**Good**	**Bad**	**Bad**	**Bad**

The preserved Greek text says "the prophets." Adding "Isaiah" is wrong because the passage refers to a quote that was not from Isaiah.

	KJV	RVG	LBA	1865	1909	1960	NVI
85	**John 1:42** which is by interpretation, **A stone.**	(que quiere decir **piedra**) • • • • • (which means **stone.**)	(que quiere decir, **Pedro**) • • • • • (which means, **Peter**)	que quiere decir, **Piedra** • • • • • which means, **Stone**	(que quiere decir, **Piedra**) • • • • • (which means, **Stone**)	(que quiere decir, **Pedro**) • • • • • (which means, **Peter**)	(es decir, **Pedro**) • • • • • (which means, **Peter**)
	Translation is... **Good**	**Good**	**Bad**	**Good but weak**	**Good but weak**	**Bad**	**Bad**

This Greek word is always translated "Peter" except here. Why? Since this verse says "which is by interpretation," the meaning must be translated, which is "a stone." Peter was "a stone" but Jesus is "the Rock." Capitalizing the word "Stone" gives emphasis on Peter.

KJV	RVG	LBA	1865	1909	1960	NVI
86						
John 3:34 for God giveth not the Spirit by measure **unto him.**	pues Dios no **le** da el Espíritu por medida. ..... God does not give the Spirit **to him** by measure.	pues Él da el Espíritu sin medida. ..... He gives the Spirit without measure.	porque no **le** da Dios el Espíritu por medida. ..... God does not give the Spirit **to him** by measure.	porque no da Dios el Espíritu por medida. ..... God does not give the Spirit by measure.	pues Dios no da el Espíritu por medida. ..... God does not give the Spirit by measure.	pues Dios mismo le da su Espíritu sin restricción. ..... God Himself gives the Spirit **to him** without restriction.
Translation is...						
Good	**Good**	**Bad**	**Good**	**Bad**	**Bad**	**Bad**

Without the words "to him or unto him," it means that God gives the Spirit without measure to all.

KJV	RVG	LBA	1865	1909	1960	NVI
87						
Romans 16:1 which is a **servant** of the church which is at Cenchrea:	es **sierva** de la iglesia ..... a **servant** of the church	**diaconisa** de la iglesia ..... a **deaconess** of the church	**en el servicio** de la iglesia ..... **in the service** of the church	es **diaconisa** de la iglesia ..... a **deaconess** of the church	es **diaconisa** de la iglesia ..... a **deaconess** of the church	**diaconisa** de la iglesia ..... **deaconess** of the church
Translation is...						
Good	**Good**	**Bad**	**Good**	**Bad**	**Bad**	**Bad**

The Greek word means "servant." Changing it to "deaconess" creates a church office that God never created, violating 1 Tim. 3:10-13.

	KJV	RVG	LBA	1865	1909	1960	NVI
88 1 John 2:28	and not be ashamed before him at his coming.	no seamos avergonzados delante de Él ..... no te be ashamed before Him	no nos apartemos de Él avergonzados ..... not separate ourselves from him ashamed	no seamos confundidos por él ..... not be con-fused by him	no seamos confundidos de él ..... not be con-fused of him	no nos alejemos de él avergonzados. ..... we move not away from him ashamed.	seguros de no ser avergonzados ..... certain of not being ashamed
Translation is...	Good	Good	Bad	Bad	Bad	Bad	Good

When Jesus comes we will not be confused "of Him" or "by Him." The 1960 and LBA add words that are not in the Greek text.

TOTAL					
KJV Good 88 Bad 0	RVG Good 88 Bad 0	LBA Good 17 Bad 71	1865 Good 51 Bad 37	1909 Good 25 Bad 63	1960 Good 12 Bad 76	NVI Good 15 Bad 73

OTHER IMPORTANT PROBLEMS WITH THE 1909 AND 1865.

1. "High priest" or "pontiff." The word "pontiff" is a Catholic word not found in the Greek or Hebrew and should have no place in the Bible. While the KJV and the RVG never use this word, the 1909 uses it 37 times and the 1865 includes it twice.

2. "Salud" or "salvation." "Salud" used to mean either "health" or "spiritual health (salvation)." But today it is used only to mean "health." The other word "salvación" has only one meaning (salvation), making it a much better choice. Unfortunately the 1909 and 1865 both use "salud" a whopping 156 times.

REINA-VALERA GÓMEZ 2010 PAPER COVER BIBLE

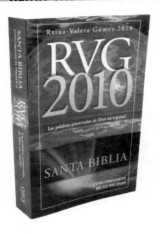

Features include:
- A 119-page concordance.
- Easy-reading typeface.
- The first Bible in Spanish not prepared by a small committee.
- Text proofread and refined by Christians in 13 countries.
- It agrees 100% with the Textus Receptus.

#262   1246 pages

Actual text size of both Bibles.

no se pierda, mas tenga vida eterna.
16 Porque de tal manera amó Dios al mundo, que ha dado a su Hijo unigénito, para que todo aquel que en Él cree, no se pierda, mas tenga vida eterna.
17 Porque no envió Dios a su Hijo al

REINA-VALERA GÓMEZ 2010 BONDED LEATHER BIBLE

Includes all the features of the Paper Cover Bible, plus:
- Smyth sewn binding for durability.
- Gold edges.
- High quality black bonded leather cover.

#1288 1246 pages